Series Edit

Love Through the Ages

Edited by Julia Geddes and Helen Ince

Oxford University Press

Great Clarendon Street, Oxford OX2 6DP

Oxford University Press is a department of the University of Oxford. It furthers the University's objective of excellence in research, scholarship, and education by publishing worldwide in

Oxford New York

Auckland Cape Town Dar es Salaam Hong Kong Karachi Kuala Lumpur Madrid Melbourne Mexico City Nairobi New Delhi Shanghai Taipei Toronto

With offices in

Argentina Austria Brazil Chile Czech Republic France Greece Guatemala Hungary Italy Japan Poland Portugal Singapore South Korea Switzerland Thailand Turkey Ukraine Vietnam

First published 2009

British Library Cataloguing in Publication Data

Data available

ISBN: 978-0-19-832880-3

1 3 5 7 9 10 8 6 4 2

Typeset in India by TNQ

Printed in China by Printplus

Paper used in the production of this book is a natural, recyclable product made from wood grown in sustainable forests. The manufacturing process conforms to the environmental regulations of the country of origin.

The publishers would like to thank the following for permission to reproduce photographs:

p2: Victoria and Albert Museum; p7: Oxford University Press; p125: Mary Evans Picture Library; p130: Getty Images; p135: Rex Features/Alastair Muir; p143: Mary Evans Picture Library; p147: Rex Features/Nils Jorgensen; p149: Getty Images/Time & Life Pictures; p153: Corbis/Benbaron Jeremy; p162: Mary Evans Picture Library

Contents

Acknowledgements

We gratefully acknowledge permission to use the following copyright texts in this book.

Vera Brittain: extract from *Testament of Youth* (Victor Gollancz, 1933), reprinted by permission of Mark Bostridge and Timothy Brittain-Catlin, literary executors for the Vera Brittain Estate, 1970.

Carol Ann Duffy: 'First Love' from *Mean Time* (Anvil, 1993), reprinted by permission of Anvil Press Poetry; and 'Pygmalion's Bride' from *The World's Wife* (Picador, 1999), reprinted by permission of Pan Macmillan, London.

Douglas Dunn: 'The Kaleidoscope' from *Elegies* (Faber, 1985), copyright © Douglas Dunn 1985, reprinted by permission of Faber & Faber Ltd.

Zelda Fitzgerald: Letter to Scott Fitzgerald from *Dear Scott, Dearest Zelda* (St Martin's Press, 2002), reprinted by permission of David Higham Associates Ltd.

John Fowles: extract from *The Collector* (Little, Brown, 1963), copyright © J.R. Fowles Ltd 1963, reprinted by permission of Aitken Alexander Associates Ltd.

Seamus Heaney: 'Clearances Sonnet 5' from *The Haw Lantern* (Faber, 1987), copyright © Seamus Heaney 1987, reprinted by permission of Faber & Faber Ltd.

Ted Hughes: 'Daffodils' from *Birthday Letters* (Faber, 1998), copyright © The Estate of Ted Hughes 1998, reprinted by permission of Faber & Faber Ltd.

Elizabeth Jennings: 'One Flesh' from *Collected Poems* (Carcanet, 1987), reprinted by permission of David Higham Associates Ltd.

Jamaica Kincaid: extract from 'My Mother' from *At the Bottom of the River* (Pan, 1984), copyright © Jamaica Kincaid 1983, reprinted by permission of The Wylie Agency, Inc.

Matthew Zapruder: extract from 'Dear X' in Joshua Knelman & Rosalind Porter (eds): *Four Letter Word – New Love Letters* (Alfred A. Knopf, 2007), reprinted by permission of the author.

We have made every effort to trace and contact copyright holders before publication. If notified, the publisher will rectify any errors or omissions at the earliest opportunity.

Acknowledgements from Julia Geddes and Helen Ince

We would like to give special thanks to Kitty Graham, for her work on some of the passages, her help, support and proofreading. Her interest and enthusiasm throughout the writing of the book was invaluable to both of us.

Editors

Steven Croft, the series editor, holds degrees from Leeds and Sheffield universities. He has taught at secondary and tertiary level and headed the Department of English and Humanities in a tertiary college. He has 25 years' examining experience at A level and is currently a Principal Examiner for English. He has written several books on teaching English at A level, and his publications for Oxford University Press include *Exploring Literature*, *Success in AQA Language and Literature* and *Exploring Language and Literature*.

Julia Geddes has a degree in English and Philosophy, and an MA in English Literature from the University of Leeds. She is currently Head of English in a large sixth form college in the north of England. She is also a Senior Examiner and Moderator and has been the author of several study guides for A level students. She presents conferences for students and provides support for teachers working with A level specifications.

Helen Ince has a degree in English Language and Literature and is currently second in department at a large sixth form college. She also works as both a Senior Examiner and Moderator, offering support and guidance for teachers of both A level English Literature and Language & Literature. She has contributed to several student workbooks, teacher guides and examination-based conferences.

Foreword

Oxford Student Texts have, over a number of years, established a reputation for presenting literary texts to students in both a scholarly and an accessible way. In response to developments in the structure and approach of A level study, several new editions have been published to help students prepare for the changing emphasis and demands of these courses. These editions have been written with a key focus on a specific area of study and contain a range of texts by a wide variety of writers intended to give a flavour of that area and provide contextual linking material that will help students develop their wider reading on a particular period or topic. Each volume in the series consists of four main sections which link together to provide an integrated approach.

The first part provides important background information about the period or thematic area and the factors that played an important part in shaping literary works. This discussion sets the various texts in context and explores some key contextual factors.

This section is followed by the texts themselves. The texts are presented without accompanying notes so that students can engage with them on their own terms without the influence of secondary ideas. To encourage this approach, the Notes are placed in the third section, immediately following the texts. The Notes provide a brief explanation of individual texts to help set them in context and also give explanations of particular words, phrases, images, allusions and so forth, to help students gain a full understanding of the particular text. They also raise questions or highlight particular issues or ideas which are important to consider when arriving at interpretations.

The fourth section, Interpretations, goes on to discuss a range of issues in more detail. This involves an examination of the influence of contextual factors as well as looking at such aspects as language and style, and various critical views or interpretations. A range of activities for students to carry out, together with discussions as to how these might be approached, are integrated into this section.

At the end of each volume there is a selection of Essay Questions, a Chronology and where appropriate a Further Reading list.

We hope you enjoy reading these texts and working with these supporting materials, and wish you every success in your studies.

Steven Croft *Series Editor*

The Literature of Love in Context

Early writers on love

Love in all its different forms has provided inspiration and subject matter for great writers across the centuries, and ideas about it have been expressed in a multitude of ways. Geoffrey Chaucer is perhaps the most celebrated writer of the early period of English literature, and love is an important theme in his work. His poem *Troilus and Criseyde* (about 1385), for example, is an account of a love affair and presents ideas about romance and relationships. Chaucer's most famous work is *The Canterbury Tales*, in which a group of pilgrims set off on their journey to Canterbury Cathedral and each one is charged with telling a tale on the way. Many of these tales are concerned with love, and they reflect a variety of views about and attitudes towards love relationships. From the courtly, chivalric love of *The Knight's Tale* to the bawdy, comic story of adultery told by the Miller (see page 17), Chaucer explores the many different forms love can take, sometimes using the tales to satirize the foolish expectations of humanity, at other times celebrating the beauty of romance and romantic ideals.

When considering the literature of the Tudor period, the sixteenth century, we can also see the many ways in which love was important in the writing of the time. It was during this era that Henry Howard, Earl of Surrey (1517–1547), introduced the unrhymed pentameters that we now call blank verse, a form that was taken up by dramatists such as William Shakespeare, Christopher Marlowe and John Webster in presenting their ideas about, among other things, love. Surrey was the first to use this form in a published work: his translation of Virgil's *Aeneid*. He was also among the first to use the sonnet form in English. Like many of his contemporaries, Surrey wrote of love as a battleground where men pursued the object of their affection but often suffered as a result of their advances being spurned. For example, in his sonnet *Love that doth reign and live within my thought*, he pictures love building *his seat within my captive breast,/Clad in the arms wherein with me he fought,/Oft in my face he doth his banner rest*. The imagery used reflects the idea of love as a war of the passions, and this is an image we see repeated throughout the period.

Poets such as Sir Thomas Wyatt (1503–1542) were also influential in the development of love poetry during this era. Wyatt was greatly influenced by the Italian writer Francesco Petrarca, known in English as Petrarch, and he is credited with introducing the Petrarchan sonnet form to English writing. In Wyatt's collection of sonnets we are offered a variety of views and complaints about love and its effects on the suffering individual. In one sonnet Wyatt uses a phrase taken directly from Petrarch, *Of Love, Fortune, and the Lover's Mind*, as the title and develops this into a complaint against the dire effects of love, writing *Love slayeth mine heart*. This sense that love is painful and challenging yet infinitely rewarding is perhaps what best characterizes the era.

The young man in this portrait miniature by Nicholas Hilliard is reminiscent of the youthful, love-sick Petrarchan lover

Though many love poems were written during the Elizabethan/Jacobean period, the sonnets of Shakespeare are perhaps some of the most famous love poetry of all time. Influenced by the work of writers such as Wyatt and Sir Philip Sidney, Shakespeare's collection of sonnets reflect a range of different views on love. Adapting the rather formal Petrarchan structure into something a little less rigid, he explored conventional love in works such as the well-known *Shall I compare thee to a summer's day* (see page 25) as well as more diverse approaches to the subject including ideas such as beauty being in the eye of the beholder, a thought explored in *My mistress' eyes are nothing like the sun*.

Many other types of love and issues surrounding the theme were explored in this era. Sir Thomas More (1478–1535), for example, considers the love of God in his *Twelve Properties or Conditions of a Lover*. Here he lists what he believes to be the demands of love on the individual, stating, for example, that the lover is *To serve his love, nothing thinking of any reward or profit*. He goes on to detail how each property should be viewed in terms of an individual's relationship with God. Clearly these properties are presented to be applied to both religious and temporal love.

Social and political influences on the presentation of love can be seen during the Tudor period. Edmund Spenser's seminal 1590 work *The Faerie Queene*, for example, is an allegorical tale of the Faerie Queene or Gloriana, who represents Elizabeth I. Book 1 of the poem is centred on the struggles of the Red Cross Knight (representing England) and his true love Una (representing the Anglican Church) against the wiles of many hostile characters (the Catholic Church and Mary Queen of Scots). The poem is deeply rooted in politics but it portrays chivalric acts of valour and the rewards of the love of a beautiful woman, illustrating the way in which the theme of love is used to present other, sometimes radical, ideas.

A golden age for drama

An important development within writing of this time was the rising popularity of tragic drama in the 1590s. The development of this form brought with it a new presentation of the theme of love. Among the earliest writers of this kind of drama was Thomas Kyd, whose *Spanish Tragedy* includes a lover's complaint against the mistress he feels unworthy of (see page 18). As with many other writers of the time, Kyd presents the woman as haughty and cold in contrast to her lover's passion and desire. Unrequited love is a common theme in writing of this period.

Although Kyd's contribution to drama was great, it was Marlowe and Shakespeare who launched the English theatre into its greatest glory. Marlowe, who was renowned for his fiery disposition, wrote several striking and successful plays before he was killed in a brawl at the age of 29. In his most famous plays, love is often presented as self-seeking, as in *Dr Faustus*, where Faustus lusts after Helen of Troy, *the face that launched a thousand ships*, and in *Edward II*, where the king's homosexual relationship with Piers Gaveston proves to be his downfall. It is left to the audience to decide how much Edward is taken in by the young man who asserts he *May draw the pliant King which way I please* (see page 19).

Shakespeare's plays also challenged the expected presentation of love. Although many of his plays follow the traditional romantic view, he created resourceful women who if necessary woo reluctant males, an image that challenges the stereotypical presentation of gender roles within courtship. The dark complexities of love are fully explored in plays such as *Othello* and *King Lear* as Shakespeare invites the audience to engage with the problems of jealousy, greed, lust and self-love. Even in those texts that could be considered traditional romances, Shakespeare constantly challenges ideas about love; comedies such *As You Like It*, *Twelfth Night* and *A Midsummer Night's Dream* set a different tone by humorously exploring the varying roles men and women play within relationships, while *Antony & Cleopatra* examines what happens when duty and politics clash with passionate love (see page 23).

Shakespeare addresses another type of love in his history plays: love of one's country. This can be seen for example in the dying John of Gaunt's speech in *Richard II* (see page 19). In his later plays, such as *The Winter's Tale*, *The Tempest* and *Pericles*, Shakespeare concerns himself with filial love, especially that between a father and daughter, and with the idea of reconciliation and healing where people who love each other have been parted or relationships have gone wrong.

In the Jacobean period dramatists such as John Webster wrote tragedies concerned with revenge, intrigue, and lust. His two most famous plays, *The White Devil* (1612) and *The Duchess of Malfi* (1614), concern themselves with violent revenge. Horrors are perpetrated on the Duchess of Malfi as punishment for defying the customs of arranged marriage and the authority of her brothers by secretly marrying the man she loves. Thomas Middleton's *The Revenger's Tragedy* (1606) is also a violent depiction of revenge, taken this time for the death of a lover.

Poets of the seventeenth century

One of the greatest poets of this era is John Donne (1572–1631), whose short love poems are characterized by sharp wit and irony as he attempts to draw meaning from his experience (see page 26). The preoccupation with questions of love, death and religious faith marks out Donne and his successors, who are often referred to as the Metaphysical poets. It is interesting to note that, though Donne's earlier work concentrates on romantic love, his later poems present the love of God in poems such as *A Hymn to God the Father.*

Also at this time we see an increase in satirical writing about love. The idea that love could be corrupted and corrupting haunted literature, but the portrayal of men idealizing women and the great love between parent and child, for example, also dominated the writing of the time. The work of the dramatist and poet Ben Jonson (1572–1637), for example, reflects these ideas. In his tender poem *On My First Daughter* (see page 27) we read not only of his pain and sorrow on losing his daughter but of his overarching belief in a benevolent God who has taken her to his care.

Another important figure in seventeenth-century English literature who founded his writing on the teachings of the Bible was John Milton. He married Mary Powell, a young woman of 17, when he was 34, and she returned to her parents a few weeks after their marriage. However, the couple were eventually reconciled and they had four children, but sadly on the birth of their daughter Deborah, Mary died. Six weeks later their 15-month-old son John also died. Milton was left bereft not just of wife and child but was also losing his sight, and in a few years he was totally blind. Milton created some of the greatest works in the English language in his head and then dictated them to his aides from memory. The most famous of his works is *Paradise Lost*, published in 1667. It depicts Satan's temptation of Eve in the Garden of Eden, and it is interesting to consider the ways Milton presents a love relationship through the images of Adam and Eve before and after their fall from God's favour. In *Paradise Lost* Book 4 he describes the pair as Satan first encounters them:

> Not equal, as their sex not equal seemed;
> For contemplation he and valour formed,
> For softness she and sweet attractive grace,
> He for God only, she for God in him
>
> (*Paradise Lost* 4:296–9)

Here we can see the biblical image of woman translated into poetry, as Milton insists on the *Absolute rule* of Adam in contrast to the subordinate role of his partner, who *Yielded with coy submission, modest pride,/And sweet reluctant amorous delay* (301, 311). It could be argued that this is every man's dream, to be heralded as the one who has complete authority and can command the submission of a beautiful woman who holds herself back with becoming modesty.

Through weakness and vanity, Milton's Eve succumbs to the temptation of Satan and in turn tempts Adam, ultimately leading to the loss of Paradise, but Milton maintains his presentation of the woman as one who is simply misguided; at the close of Book 12 the couple are reconciled to each other and their loss, as they *hand in hand with wandering steps and slow,/Through Eden took their solitary way*. However, the image of woman as a temptress likely to lure a man away from his pure and spiritual self can be found in literature throughout the ages; Thomas Hardy is among those who expose the injustice of this concept, in for example *Tess of the d'Urbervilles*, as do many contemporary writers.

This 1504 engraving of Adam and Eve by Albrecht Dürer shows the temptation of Adam

Romantic literature and the Victorian era

The eighteenth and early nineteenth centuries are characterized as the Age of Enlightenment, a time when philosophical thinking and new ideas on politics and religion dominated. Though writers of the time often strived to reflect and challenge these new philosophies, the theme of love still prevailed in literature. Authors such as Mary Shelley and Nathaniel Hawthorne explored ideas about the changing moral structure of the modern world but often portrayed their ideas through relationships; Shelley's novel *Frankenstein* (1818), for example, considers the progress of science and challenges ideas about the human soul, but at its heart is the traumatic, destructive search for love by Frankenstein's monstrous creation.

The Romantic poets, writers such as William Blake, S.T. Coleridge and William Wordsworth, did not, as the term may suggest, simply write about romance. They were interested in love of the landscape and often tried to capture in their writing a feeling of the sublime and an overwhelming passion for nature and for God. Works such as Coleridge's *Lines composed while climbing the left ascent of Brockley Coomb* (see page 30) and Wordsworth's *Lines composed a few miles above Tintern Abbey*, for example, both explore the love of nature with the enthusiasm that typifies the Romantic movement. Though many other poems of the age can be seen to reflect traditional ideals about love (Coleridge's 1796 poem *The Eolian Harp*, for example), many writers of the time used their craft to foreground a love of the countryside.

Queen Victoria came to the throne in 1837, and in the Victorian era the Industrial Revolution brought widespread social change and great expansion in the British economy. With this increased wealth and mobility, alliances through marriage became an important means of maintaining a family's inheritance and status. As a result, courtship and marriage conventions became rather regimented and instead of focusing on love alone, the writing of the time tended to deal with the way relationships adapted to these conventions. Strict social codes made falling in love with an 'unsuitable' person problematic, and even where the partnership was considered socially acceptable, complex conventions of courtship had to be adhered to, among the more prosperous classes at least. In particular, there was a strict set of rules that governed the way in which a single woman must behave. She would not, for example, be able to travel in a closed carriage with a man unless he was a relative. Nor would she be allowed to address a single man without introduction by a third party, and she would always be chaperoned when in his company. The presentation of love in the literature of the time is therefore interesting for what it tells us about the social climate, the role of women and the division of the classes, for example.

The development of the novel in this era added a new dimension to the ways in which love was presented. The publication of extended stories in magazines as well as the rise in popularity of libraries, which lent copies of the latest novels, brought the novel form to a wider audience and gave writers the chance to explore a broader range of situations and views. The Brontë sisters challenged the stereotypes of romance in their work by creating determined and passionate heroines such as Jane Eyre, who, in Charlotte Brontë's novel of that name (see page 36), refuses to conform to the stereotype of the weak female rescued by a man. Brontë's unlikely heroine leaves Edward Rochester (and rejects another suitor's offer of marriage) and instead seeks independence. It is only when she becomes financially independent and Rochester, blinded in a fire, must depend on her that she returns to her true love. While this is the kind of romantic love the Victorians enjoyed reading about, it does not necessarily reflect the realities of the time for the majority of people, when love often had to be worked towards within marriages that were entered into for more material reasons. It is perhaps important to note here that it has often been suggested that the ending of *Jane Eyre* (see Interpretations, page 134) was altered to please the Victorian reader and that Brontë had originally concluded the novel with Jane alone and independent.

Other female writers of the time were also beginning to challenge the way in which women and love were presented. Poets such as Elizabeth Barrett Browning and Christina Rossetti, for example, were exploring the issue of love and marriage by considering the sacrifice of individualism that had to be made by women if they were to become wives. In her poem *Aurora Leigh* (1856), Barrett Browning's heroine struggles for an independent life and the poet seems to be suggesting that to be married is to give up all freedom. Her main concern was that a loss of freedom would lead to a loss of creativity and individuality. It is important to note, however, that although many poems seem to reflect a preoccupation with the fear of love as something that will defeat the individual, Barrett Browning also created some of the most eloquent love poems, in her *Sonnets from the Portuguese* (1850) where she expresses her love for the poet Robert Browning and reflects on elements of their courtship. Similarly, Rossetti's poetry reflects her fear that marriage would be a restriction. More poignant, however, is the way in which Rossetti often associated love with death, and there is a sense of melancholy in her love poems (see page 37).

Many late Victorian writers questioned well-established social and economic customs, and the presentation of love in literature from the latter half of the century often challenged traditional views of marriage in a more drastic way. Oscar Wilde's 1893 play *A Woman of No Importance*, for example, champions the 'fallen woman' and questions society's views about sex outside marriage (see page 40). Whereas previous literature had focused on courtship and often celebrated the idea of a happy, monogamous and heterosexual marriage, Wilde's writings often explored atypical love. Wilde was considered one of the new radicals and his literature reflects a changing perception of love that included quite direct criticism of the institution of marriage and an interest in those who challenged social norms.

Modern and post-modern writing

As the economic and cultural expansion of the Victorian age came to a close, and particularly after the end of the First World War in 1918, the modern era promoted radical thinking and a change in political and social consciousness from the stoicism of the earlier years. The rise of Marxist ideologies, feminism and the growing interest in the work of psycho-analysts such as Sigmund Freud meant that the social climate was fast-changing. Increased social mobility and technological developments were reflected in more liberal, often controversial, literary works. A more diverse range of topics were taken up in literature, but love remained a fascinating subject that appealed to readers and was still important to all the literary genres.

The First World War had an enormous impact on the literature of the time. A wide range of writings depict the horror and grief caused by the war, but there are many examples of writing from a variety of genres (poetry, prose and non-fiction in particular) that focus on the theme of love. Many of these pieces illustrate the changing relationship between men and women during these years as the deployment of so many men to the battlefields meant women were forced to become more independent; this undoubtedly impacted on the relationships between the genders.

The creation of the 'modern novel' is often attributed to writers such as Virginia Woolf and James Joyce, and with the development of techniques such as the stream of consciousness in prose and free verse in poetry, writers reflected their thoughts and feelings in a more versatile way. In Woolf's *Mrs Dalloway* (1925) for example, we enter the mind of the protagonist Clarissa through a stream of consciousness. She reflects on her 'sensible' choice of husband – she selected the rather dull but financially stable and socially reliable Richard, rather than following her heart. Like previous presentations of love through the ages, Woolf reflects the way in which social issues impact on our experience of relationships. By presenting Clarissa's plight through a fragmented narrative that directly illustrates the way in which she is thinking, Woolf draws readers in and allows them to experience Clarissa's inner turmoil.

In post-modern literature (in general terms, that written since the Second World War) a more liberal social climate and freedom from censorship have influenced writing on love, leading to a range of tones; certainly there is no longer seen to be a need for a happy ending to a love story. John Fowles's *The Collector*, for example (see page 46) is a disturbing presentation of obsession, and depicts the deranged behaviour such obsession can lead to. Fowles's book challenges the reader's perception of relationships, as does Jeanette Winterson's exploration of lesbian love, *Oranges Are Not the Only Fruit* (1985). This semi-autobiographical narrative confronts stereotypes as it follows the young protagonist's journey of sexual discovery, and Winterson uses her central character's simple, innocent views on love as a contrast to the rather brutal, bigoted opinions of her fanatically religious mother. The novel challenges traditional religious views that homosexuality is a sin while at the same time celebrating difference and championing love in a different form.

Poets such as Sylvia Plath and Simon Armitage also offer contemporary, critical views of relationships, and realistic presentations of love can be seen in collections such as Plath's *Ariel* and Armitage's *The Dead Sea Poems*. While both collections can be seen to explore ideas from an autobiographical viewpoint, they do so very differently. Plath, struggling to deal with her psychological instability and depression, explores the pain of being unable to love and be loved. In her poem *Elm*, Plath comments that *Love is a shadow* and goes on to describe her fear of *this dark thing/That sleeps in me*, almost as if her inability to love haunts her. A striking presentation of the pain of loss is given in *Daddy*, where she explores the devastating impact her father's death had upon her. Describing her own suicide attempt as a way to get back to him, she laments that *I thought even the bones would do*. Armitage, on the other hand, focuses more on the strength that familial love can provide, as well as exploring the importance of finding your own identity and being comfortable with who you are as an individual before you can build meaningful relationships with others. His poem *Hipflask*, for example, uses the simple image of a hipflask as a token to represent the love, one that we can carry with us wherever we are. He describes the object in practical terms throughout the poem and it seems unrelated to anything more emotional until the final lines take up the hint in line 3, where it is introduced as *this gift*, and describe it as a *present made/to hide the heart and hold the heart in place*. Armitage seems to be suggesting that the ramifications of love can be found in the most ordinary places.

Carol Ann Duffy's poetry also often reflects on different types of love. Her collection *Standing Female Nude* looks at, among other things, issues to do with social perceptions of beauty and sexuality, and *The World's Wife* and *Mean Time* present some challenging views of relationships and female identity (see pages 50 and 53).

In the literature of today, love is still a central topic of creative writing. From the haunting images of dutiful, challenging love in *The Kite Runner* by Khaled Hosseini to the various humorous relationships in the works of Zadie Smith, love is a core theme. Although it can be seen as we look through the ages that the purpose of presenting love and the types of love in literature across different literary eras may change, the sense that it is a fundamental part of the human condition remains a constant. The fact that it can challenge, liberate, damage and inspire all of us makes love perhaps the most enthralling aspect of writing in literature old and new.

Love
Through the Ages

The Miller's Tale: Geoffrey Chaucer

Now, sire, and eft, sire, so bifel the cas
That on a day this hende Nicholas
Fil with this yonge wyf to rage and pleye,
Whil that hir housbonde was at Oseneye,
As clerkes ben ful subtile and ful queynte;
And prively he caughte hire by the queynte,
And seyde, 'Ywis, but if ich have my wille,
For deerne love of thee, lemman, I spille.'
And heeld hire harde by the haunchebones,
And seyde, 'Lemman, love me al atones,
Or I wol dyen, also God me save!'
And she sproong as a colt dooth in the trave,
And with hir heed she wryed faste awey,
And seyde, 'I wol nat kisse thee, by my fey!
Why, lat be!' quod she. 'Lat be, Nicholas,
Or I wol crie "out, harrow" and "allas"!
Do wey youre handes, for youre curteisye!'
　　This Nicholas gan mercy for to crye,
And spak so faire, and profred him so faste,
That she hir love hym graunted atte laste,
And swoor hir ooth, by Seint Thomas of Kent,
That she wol been at his comandement,
Whan that she may hir leyser wel espie.
'Myn housbonde is so ful of jalousie
That but ye wayte wel and been privee,
I woot right wel I nam but deed,' quod she.
'Ye moste been ful deerne, as in this cas.'
　　'Nay, therof care thee noght,' quod Nicholas.
'A clerk hadde litherly biset his whyle,
But if he koude a carpenter bigyle.'
And thus they been accorded and ysworn
To wayte a tyme, as I have told biforn.

Whan Nicholas had doon thus everideel
And thakked hire aboute the lendes weel,
He kiste hire sweete and taketh his sawtrie,
And pleyeth faste, and maketh melodie.

The Spanish Tragedy: Thomas Kyd

BALTHAZAR No, she is wilder, and more hard withal,
Than beast, or bird, or tree, or stony wall.
But wherefore blot I Bellimperia's name?
It is my fault, not she, that merits blame.
My feature is not to content her sight,
My words are rude, and work her no delight.
The lines I send her are but harsh and ill,
Such as do drop from Pan and Marsyas' quill.
My presents are not of sufficient cost,
And being worthless, all my labour's lost.
Yet might she love me for my valiancy;
Ay, but that's slander'd by captivity.
Yet might she love me to content her sire:
Ay, but her reason masters his desire.
Yet might she love me as her brother's friend:
Ay, but her hopes aim at some other end.
Yet might she love me to uprear her state:
Ay, but perhaps she hopes some nobler mate.
Yet might she love me as her beauty's thrall:
Ay, but I fear she cannot love at all.

Edward II: Christopher Marlowe

GAVESTON I must have wanton poets, pleasant wits
Musicians, that with touching of a string
May draw the pliant King which way I please.
Music and poetry is his delight;
Therefore I'll have Italian masques by night,
Sweet speeches, comedies, and pleasing shows;
And in the day when he shall walk abroad,
Like sylvan nymphs my pages shall be clad,
My men like satyrs grazing on the lawns
Shall with their goat-feet dance an antic hay;
Sometime a lovely boy in Dian's shape,
With hair that gilds the water as it glides,
Crownets of pearl about his naked arms,
And in his sportful hands an olive tree
To hide those parts which men delight to see,
Shall bathe him in a spring; and there hard by,
One like Actaeon peeping through the grove,
Shall by the angry goddess be transformed,
And running in the likeness of an hart,
By yelping hounds pulled down, and seem to die.
Such things as these best please his majesty.

Richard II: William Shakespeare

JOHN OF GAUNT Methinks I am a prophet new inspired
And thus expiring do foretell of him:
His rash fierce blaze of riot cannot last,
For violent fires soon burn out themselves;
Small showers last long, but sudden storms are short;
He tires betimes that spurs too fast betimes;
With eager feeding food doth choke the feeder:

Light vanity, insatiate cormorant,
Consuming means, soon preys upon itself.
This royal throne of kings, this scepter'd isle,
This earth of majesty, this seat of Mars,
This other Eden, demi-paradise,
This fortress built by Nature for herself
Against infection and the hand of war,
This happy breed of men, this little world,
This precious stone set in the silver sea,
Which serves it in the office of a wall,
Or as a moat defensive to a house,
Against the envy of less happier lands,
This blessed plot, this earth, this realm, this England,
This nurse, this teeming womb of royal kings,
Fear'd by their breed and famous by their birth,
Renowned for their deeds as far from home,
For Christian service and true chivalry,
As is the sepulchre in stubborn Jewry,
Of the world's ransom, blessed Mary's Son,
This land of such dear souls, this dear dear land,
Dear for her reputation through the world,
Is now leased out, I die pronouncing it,
Like to a tenement or pelting farm:
England, bound in with the triumphant sea
Whose rocky shore beats back the envious siege
Of watery Neptune, is now bound in with shame,
With inky blots and rotten parchment bonds:
That England, that was wont to conquer others,
Hath made a shameful conquest of itself.
Ah, would the scandal vanish with my life,
How happy then were my ensuing death!

Henry V: William Shakespeare

KING HENRY V God's peace! I would not lose so great an honour
As one man more, methinks, would share from me,
For the best hope I have. O do not wish one more!
Rather proclaim it, Westmorland, through my host,
That he which hath no stomach to this fight,
Let him depart; his passport shall be made
And crowns for convoy put into his purse.
We would not die in that man's company
That fears his fellowship to die with us.
This day is called the feast of Crispian.
He that outlives this day, and comes safe home
Will stand a-tiptoe when the day is named
And rouse him at the name of Crispian.
He that shall see this day and live old age,
Will yearly on the vigil feast his neighbours,
And say 'Tomorrow is Saint Crispian.'
Then will he strip his sleeve and show his scars,
And say 'These wounds I had on Crispin's day.'
Old men forget; yet all shall be forgot
But he'll remember, with advantages,
What feats he did that day. Then shall our names,
Familiar in his mouth as household words,
Harry the King, Bedford and Exeter,
Warwick and Talbot, Salisbury and Gloucester,
Be in their flowing cups freshly remembered.
This story shall the good man teach his son,
And Crispin Crispian shall ne'er go by
From this day to the ending of the world
But we in it shall be remembered,
We few, we happy few, we band of brothers.
For he today that sheds his blood with me

Shall be my brother; be he ne'er so vile,
This day shall gentle his condition.
And gentlemen in England now abed
Shall think themselves accursed they were not here,
And hold their manhoods cheap whiles any speaks
That fought with us upon Saint Crispin's day.

Much Ado About Nothing: William Shakespeare

CLAUDIO O, my lord,
When you went onward on this ended action,
I look'd upon her with a soldier's eye,
That liked, but had a rougher task in hand
Than to drive liking to the name of love:
But now I am return'd and that war-thoughts
Have left their places vacant, in their rooms
Come thronging soft and delicate desires,
All prompting me how fair young Hero is,
Saying, I liked her ere I went to wars.
DON PEDRO Thou wilt be like a lover presently
And tire the hearer with a book of words.
If thou dost love fair Hero, cherish it,
And I will break with her and with her father,
And thou shalt have her. Was't not to this end
That thou began'st to twist so fine a story?
CLAUDIO How sweetly you do minister to love,
That know love's grief by his complexion!
But lest my liking might too sudden seem,
I would have salved it with a longer treatise.
DON PEDRO What need the bridge much broader than the flood?
The fairest grant is the necessity.

Look, what will serve is fit: 'tis once, thou lovest,
And I will fit thee with the remedy.
I know we shall have revelling to-night:
I will assume thy part in some disguise
And tell fair Hero I am Claudio,
And in her bosom I'll unclasp my heart
And take her hearing prisoner with the force
And strong encounter of my amorous tale:
Then after to her father will I break;
And the conclusion is, she shall be thine.
In practise let us put it presently.
Exeunt

Antony & Cleopatra: William Shakespeare

Enter Demetrius and Philo

PHILO Nay, but this dotage of our general's
O'erflows the measure. Those his goodly eyes,
That o'er the files and musters of the war
Have glow'd like plated Mars, now bend, now turn
The office and devotion of their view
Upon a tawny front. His captain's heart,
Which in the scuffles of great fights hath burst
The buckles on his breast, reneges all temper
And is become the bellows and the fan
To cool a gipsy's lust.
Flourish. Enter Antony, Cleopatra, her Ladies, the Train, with Eunuchs fanning her
Look, where they come!
Take but good note, and you shall see in him
The triple pillar of the world transformed
Into a strumpet's fool. Behold and see.

CLEOPATRA If it be love indeed, tell me how much.
ANTONY There's beggary in the love that can be reckoned.
CLEOPATRA I'll set a bourn how far to be beloved.
ANTONY Then must thou needs find out new heaven,
new earth.

Enter a Messenger

MESSENGER News, my good lord, from Rome.
ANTONY Grates me! The sum.
CLEOPATRA Nay, hear them, Antony.
Fulvia perchance is angry, or who knows
If the scarce-bearded Caesar have not sent
His powerful mandate to you: 'Do this, or this;
Take in that kingdom, and enfranchise that;
Perform't, or else we damn thee.'
ANTONY How, my love?
CLEOPATRA Perchance? Nay, and most like.
You must not stay here longer; your dismission
Is come from Caesar; therefore hear it, Antony.
Where's Fulvia's process? – Caesar's, I would say? Both?
Call in the messengers! As I am Egypt's Queen,
Thou blushest, Antony, and that blood of thine
Is Caesar's homager; else so thy cheek pays shame
When shrill-tongued Fulvia scolds. The messengers!
ANTONY Let Rome in Tiber melt, and the wide arch
Of the ranged empire fall! Here is my space!
Kingdoms are clay! Our dungy earth alike
Feeds beast as man. The nobleness of life
Is to do thus, when such a mutual pair
And such a twain can do't, in which I bind,
On pain of punishment, the world to weet
We stand up peerless.
CLEOPATRA Excellent falsehood!
Why did he marry Fulvia, and not love her?
I'll seem the fool I am not; Antony

Will be himself.
ANTONY But stirred by Cleopatra.
Now, for the love of Love and her soft hours,
Let's not confound the time with conference harsh.
There's not a minute of our lives should stretch
Without some pleasure now. What sport tonight?
CLEOPATRA Hear the ambassadors.
ANTONY Fie, wrangling queen,
Whom everything becomes – to chide, to laugh,
To weep; whose every passion fully strives
To make itself, in thee, fair and admired!
No messenger but thine, and all alone
Tonight we'll wander through the streets and note
The qualities of people. Come, my queen!
Last night you did desire it. (*To the Messenger*) Speak not to us.
Exeunt Antony and Cleopatra with their train

Sonnet 18: William Shakespeare

Shall I compare thee to a summer's day?
Thou art more lovely and more temperate:
Rough winds do shake the darling buds of May,
And summer's lease hath all too short a date;
Sometime too hot the eye of heaven shines,
And often is his gold complexion dimmed,
And every fair from fair sometime declines,
By chance or nature's changing course untrimmed:
But thy eternal summer shall not fade,
Nor lose possession of that fair thou ow'st;
Nor shall Death brag thou wand'rest in his shade,
When in eternal lines to time thou grow'st.
So long as men can breathe or eyes can see,
So long lives this, and this gives life to thee.

A Valediction: Forbidding Mourning: John Donne

As virtuous men pass mildly away,
	And whisper to their souls, to go,
Whilst some of their sad friends do say,
	The breath goes now, and some say, no:

So let us melt, and make no noise,
	No tear-floods, nor sigh-tempests move,
'Twere profanation of our joys
	To tell the laity our love.

Moving of th' earth brings harms and fears,
	Men reckon what it did and meant,
But trepidation of the spheres,
	Though greater far, is innocent.

Dull sublunary lovers' love
	(Whose soul is sense) cannot admit
Absence, because it doth remove
	Those things which elemented it.

But we by a love, so much refined,
	That our selves know not what it is,
Inter-assured of the mind,
	Care less, eyes, lips and hands to miss.

Our two souls therefore, which are one,
	Though I must go, endure not yet
A breach, but an expansion,
	Like gold to aery thinness beat.

If they be two, they are two so
    As stiff twin compasses are two,
Thy soul the fixed foot, makes no show
    To move, but doth, if th'other do.

And though it in the centre sit,
    Yet when the other far doth roam,
It leans, and hearkens after it,
    And grows erect, as that comes home.

Such wilt thou be to me, who must
    Like th' other foot, obliquely run;
Thy firmness makes my circle just,
    And makes me end, where I begun.

On My First Daughter: Ben Jonson

Here lies to each her parents' ruth,
Mary, the daughter of their youth:
Yet, all heaven's gifts, being heaven's due,
It makes the father, less, to rue.
At six months' end, she parted hence
With safety of her innocence;
Whose soul heaven's queen, (whose name she bears)
In comfort of her mother's tears,
Hath placed amongst her virgin train:
Where, while that severed doth remain,
This grave partakes the fleshly birth.
Which cover lightly, gentle earth.

'Tis Pity She's a Whore: John Ford

GIOVANNI Lost, I am lost: my fates have doomed my death.
The more I strive, I love; the more I love,
The less I hope. I see my ruin, certain.
What judgement or endeavours could apply
To my incurable and restless wounds
I throughly have examined, but in vain.
O that it were not in religion sin
To make our love a god, and worship it!
I have even wearied Heaven with prayers, dried up
The spring of my continual tears, even starved
My veins with daily fasts: what wit or art
Could counsel, I have practised. But alas,
I find all these but dreams, and old men's tales
To fright unsteady youth: I'm still the same.
Or I must speak, or burst. 'Tis not, I know,
My lust, but 'tis my fate that leads me on.
Keep fear and low, faint-hearted shame with slaves!
I'll tell her that I love her, though my heart
Were rated at the price of that attempt.
Enter Annabella and Putana
O me! She comes.
ANNABELLA Brother.
GIOVANNI (*Aside*) If such a thing
As courage dwell in men, ye heavenly powers,
Now double all that virtue in my tongue.
ANNABELLA Why brother, will you not speak to me?
GIOVANNI Yes; how d'ee, sister?
ANNABELLA Howsoever I am, methinks you are not well.
PUTANA Bless us, why are you so sad, sir?
GIOVANNI Let me entreat you leave us awhile, Putana.

Sister, I would be private with you.
ANNABELLA Withdraw, Putana.
PUTANA I will. (*Aside*) If this were any other company for her, I should think my absence an office of some credit; but I will leave them together. *Exit*
GIOVANNI Come sister, lend your hand, let's walk together.
I hope you need not blush to walk with me;
Here's none but you and I.

Deo Salvatori: Thomas Fettiplace

With sighing soul and bended knee
Thy servant vows himself to Thee:
My God, accept a broken heart
Bleeding for sin; O Thou which art
The sovereign balm, vouchsafe to be
(My dearest Lord) that balm to me.
Inlighten with Thy saving grace,
Those eyes Thou guidest to this place
And grant (dear God) those sins of mine
May not obscure that grace of Thine.

The Clod and the Pebble: William Blake

'Love seeketh not itself to please,
Nor for itself hath any care,
But for another gives its ease,
And builds a Heaven in Hell's despair.'

So sung a little Clod of Clay,
Trodden with the cattle's feet,

But a Pebble of the brook
Warbled out these metres meet:

'Love seeketh only self to please,
To bind another to its delight,
Joys in another's loss of ease,
And builds a Hell in Heaven's despite.'

Lines composed while climbing the left ascent of Brockley Coomb: S.T. Coleridge

With many a pause and oft reverted eye
I climb the Coomb's ascent: sweet songsters near
Warble in shade their wild-wood melody:
Far off th' unvarying Cuckoo soothes my ear.
Up scour the startling stragglers of the Flock
That on green plots o'er precipices browse:
From the forc'd fissures of the naked rock
The Yew tree bursts! Beneath its dark green boughs
('Mid which the May-thorn blends its blossoms white)
Where broad smooth stones jut out in mossy seats,
I rest: – And now have gain'd the topmost site.
Ah! what a luxury of landscape meets
My gaze! Proud Towers, and Cots more dear to me,
Elm-shadow'd Fields, and prospect-bounding Sea!
Deep sighs my lonely heart: I drop the tear:
Enchanting spot! O were my Sara here!

The First Tooth: Mary Lamb

SISTER
Through the house what busy joy,
Just because the infant boy
Has a tiny tooth to show.
I have got a double row,
All as white, and all as small;
Yet no one cares for mine at all.
He can say but half a word,
Yet that single sound's preferred
To all the words that I can say
In the longest summer day.
He cannot walk, yet if he put
With mimic motion out his foot,
As if he thought he were advancing,
It's prized more than my best dancing.

BROTHER
Sister, I know, you jesting are,
Yet O! of jealousy beware.
If the smallest seed should be
In your mind of jealousy,
It will spring, and it will shoot,
Till it bear the baneful fruit.
I remember you, my dear,
Young as is this infant here.
There was not a tooth of those
Your pretty even ivory rows,
But as anxiously was watched,
Till it burst its shell new hatched,
As if it a Phoenix were,
Or some other wonder rare.
So when you began to walk –

So when you began to talk –
As now, the same encomiums past.
'Tis not fitting this should last
Longer than our infant days;
A child is fed with milk and praise.

The Eve of St Agnes: John Keats

XXX
And still she slept an azure-lidded sleep,
In blanchèd linen, smooth, and lavendered,
While he from forth the closet brought a heap
Of candied apple, quince, and plum, and gourd,
With jellies soother than the creamy curd,
And lucent syrups, tinct with cinnamon;
Manna and dates, in argosy transferred
From Fez; and spicèd dainties, every one,
From silken Samarkand to cedared Lebanon.

XXXI
These delicates he heaped with glowing hand
On golden dishes and in baskets bright
Of wreathèd silver; sumptuous they stand
In the retired quiet of the night,
Filling the chilly room with perfume light.
'And now, my love, my seraph fair, awake!
Thou art my heaven, and I thine eremite:
Open thine eyes, for meek St Agnes' sake,
Or I shall drowse beside thee, so my soul doth ache.'

XXXII
Thus whispering, his warm, unnervèd arm
Sank in her pillow. Shaded was her dream

By the dusk curtains – 'twas a midnight charm
Impossible to melt as iced stream:
The lustrous salvers in the moonlight gleam;
Broad golden fringe upon the carpet lies.
It seemed he never, never could redeem
From such a steadfast spell his lady's eyes;
So mused awhile, entoiled in woofèd fantasies.

XXXIII

Awakening up, he took her hollow lute,
Tumultuous, and, in chords that tenderest be,
He played an ancient ditty, long since mute,
In Provence called, 'La belle dame sans mercy':
Close to her ear touching the melody –
Wherewith disturbed, she uttered a soft moan:
He ceased – she panted quick – and suddenly
Her blue affrayèd eyes wide open shone.
Upon his knees he sank, pale as smooth-sculptured
stone.

XXXIV

Her eyes were open, but she still beheld,
Now wide awake, the vision of her sleep –
There was a painful change, that nigh expelled
The blisses of her dream so pure and deep.
At which fair Madeline began to weep,
And moan forth witless words with many a sigh,
While still her gaze on Porphyro would keep;
Who knelt, with joinèd hands and piteous eye,
Fearing to move or speak, she looked so dreamingly.

XXXV

'Ah, Porphyro!' said she, 'but even now
Thy voice was at sweet tremble in mine ear,

Made tuneable with every sweetest vow,
And those sad eyes were spiritual and clear:
How changed thou art! How pallid, chill, and drear!
Give me that voice again, my Porphyro,
Those looks immortal, those complainings dear!
O leave me not in this eternal woe,
For if thou diest, my Love, I know not where to go.'

XXXVI

Beyond a mortal man impassioned far
At these voluptuous accents, he arose,
Ethereal, flushed, and like a throbbing star
Seen mid the sapphire heaven's deep repose;
Into her dream he melted, as the rose
Blendeth its odour with the violet –
Solution sweet. Meantime the frost-wind blows
Like Love's alarum pattering the sharp sleet
Against the window-panes; St Agnes' moon hath set.

Letter to Fanny Brawne: John Keats

Wednesday Morng.

My dearest Girl,

I have been a walk this morning with a book in my hand, but as usual I have been occupied with nothing but you: I wish I could say in an agreeable manner. I am tormented day and night. They talk of my going to Italy. 'Tis certain I shall never recover if I am to be so long separate from you; yet with all this devotion to you I cannot persuade myself into any confidence of you. Past experience connected with the fact of my long separation from you gives me agonies which are scarcely to be talked of. When your mother comes I shall be very sudden and expert in asking her whether you have been to Mrs Dilke's, for she might say no to make me easy. I am literally worn to death, which seems my only recourse. I cannot forget what has pass'd. What? nothing with a man of the world, but to me deathful. I will get rid of this as much as possible. When you were in the habit of flirting with Brown you would have left off, could your own heart have felt one half of one pang mine did. Brown is a good sort of Man – he did not know he was doing me to death by inches. I feel the effect of every one of those hours in my side now; and for that cause, though he has done me many services, though I know his love and friendship for me, though at this moment I should be without pence were it not for his assistance, I will never see or speak to him until we are both old men, if we are to be. I *will* resent my heart having been made a football. You will call this madness. I have heard you say that it was not unpleasant to wait a few years – you have amusements – your mind is away – you have not brooded over one idea as I have, and how should you? You are to me an object intensely desireable – the air I breathe in a room empty of you is unhealthy. I am not the same to you – no – you can wait – you have a thousand activities – you can be happy without me. Any party, any thing to fill up the day has been enough. How have you pass'd this month? Who have you smil'd with? All this may seem savage in me. You do not feel as I do – you do not know what it is to love – one day you may – your time is not come. Ask yourself how many unhappy hours Keats has caused you in Loneliness. For myself I have been a Martyr the whole time, and for this reason I speak; the confession is forc'd from me by the torture. I appeal to you by the blood of that Christ you believe in: Do not write to me if you have done anything this month which it would have pained me to have seen. You may have altered – if you have not – if you still behave in dancing rooms and other societies as I have seen you – I do not want to live – if you have done so I wish this coming night may be my last. I cannot live without, and not only you but *chaste you; virtuous you.* The Sun rises and sets, the day passes, and you follow the bent of your inclination to a certain extent – you have no conception of the quantity of miserable feeling that passes through me in a day. – Be serious! Love is not a plaything – and again do not write unless you can do it with a crystal conscience. I would sooner die for want of you than –

Yours for ever
J. Keats

Jane Eyre: Charlotte Brontë

My tale draws to its close: one word respecting my experience of married life, and one brief glance at the fortunes of those whose names have most frequently recurred in this narrative, and I have done.

I have now been married ten years. I know what it is to live entirely for and with what I love best on earth. I hold myself supremely blest – blest beyond what language can express; because I am my husband's life as fully is he is mine. No woman was ever nearer to her mate than I am: ever more absolutely bone of his bone and flesh of his flesh. I know no weariness of my Edward's society: he knows none of mine, any more than we each do of the pulsation of the heart that beats in our separate bosoms; consequently, we are ever together. To be together is for us to be at once as free as in solitude, as gay as in company. We talk, I believe, all day long: to talk to each other is but a more animated and an audible thinking. All my confidence is bestowed on him, all his confidence is devoted to me; we are precisely suited in character – perfect concord is the result.

Mr Rochester continued blind the first two years of our union: perhaps it was that circumstance that drew us so very near – that knit us so very close: for I was then his vision, as I am still his right hand. Literally, I was (what he often called me) the apple of his eye. He saw nature – he saw books through me; and never did I weary of gazing for his behalf, and of putting into words, the effect of field, tree, town, river, cloud, sunbeam – of the landscape before us; of the weather round us – and impressing by sound on his ear what light could no longer stamp on his eye. Never did I weary of reading to him; never did I weary of conducting him where he wished to go: of doing for him what he wished to be done. And there was a pleasure in my services, most full, most exquisite, even though sad – because he claimed these services without painful shame or damping humiliation. He loved me so truly that he knew no reluctance in profiting by my attendance; he felt I loved him so fondly, that to yield that attendance was to indulge my sweetest wishes.

Remember: Christina Rossetti

Remember me when I am gone away,
    Gone far away into the silent land;
    When you can no more hold me by the hand,
Nor I half turn to go, yet turning stay.
Remember me when no more day by day
    You tell me of our future that you planned:
    Only remember me; you understand

It will be late to counsel then or pray.
Yet if you should forget me for a while
And afterwards remember, do not grieve:
For if the darkness and corruption leave
A vestige of the thoughts that once I had,
Better by far you should forget and smile
Than that you should remember and be sad.

Middlemarch: George Eliot

It had now entered Dorothea's mind that Mr Casaubon might wish to make her his wife, and the idea that he would do so touched her with a sort of reverential gratitude. How good of him – nay, it would be almost as if a winged messenger had suddenly stood beside her path and held out his hand towards her! For a long while she had been oppressed by the indefiniteness which hung in her mind, like a thick summer haze, over all her desire to make her life greatly effective. What could she do, what ought she to do? – she, hardly more than a budding woman, but yet with an active conscience and a great mental need, not to be satisfied by a girlish instruction comparable to the nibblings and judgments of a discursive mouse. With some endowment of stupidity and conceit, she might have thought that a Christian young lady of fortune should find her ideal of life in village charities, patronage of the humbler clergy, the perusal of 'Female Scripture Characters,' unfolding the private experience of Sara under the Old Dispensation, and Dorcas under the New, and the care of her soul over her embroidery in her own boudoir – with a background of prospective marriage to a man who, if less strict than herself, as being involved in affairs religiously inexplicable, might be prayed for and seasonably exhorted. From such contentment poor Dorothea was shut out. The intensity of her religious disposition, the coercion it exercised over her life, was but one aspect of a nature altogether ardent, theoretic, and intellectually consequent: and with such a nature, struggling in the bands of a narrow teaching, hemmed in by a social life which seemed nothing but a labyrinth of petty courses, a walled-in maze of small paths that led no whither, the outcome was sure to strike others as at once exaggeration and inconsistency. The thing which seemed to her best, she wanted to justify by the completest knowledge; and not to live in a pretended admission of rules which were never acted on. Into this soul-hunger as yet all her youthful passion was poured; the union which attracted her was one that would deliver her from her girlish subjection to her own ignorance, and give her the freedom of voluntary submission to a guide who would take her along the grandest path.

'I should learn everything then,' she said to herself, still walking quickly along the bridle road through the wood. 'It would be my duty to study that I might help him the better in his great works. There would be nothing trivial about our lives. Everyday things with us would mean the greatest things. It would be like marrying Pascal. I should learn to see the truth by the same light as great men have seen it by. And then I should know what to do, when I got older: I should see how it was possible to lead a grand life here – now – in England. I don't feel sure about doing good in any way now: everything seems like going on a mission to a people whose language I don't know; – unless it were building good cottages – there can be no doubt about that. Oh, I hope I should be able to get the people well housed in Lowick! I will draw plenty of plans while I have time.'

A Woman of No Importance: Oscar Wilde

GERALD Mother, tell me what Lord Illingworth did? If he did anything shameful, I will not go away with him. Surely you know me well enough for that?

MRS ARBUTHNOT Gerald, come near to me. Quite close to me, as you used to do when you were a little boy, when you were mother's own boy. (*Gerald sits down beside his mother. She runs her fingers through his hair, and strokes his hands.*) Gerald, there was a girl once, she was very young, she was little over eighteen at the time. George Harford – that was Lord Illingworth's name then – George Harford met her. She knew nothing about life. He – knew everything. He made this girl love him. He made her love him so much that she left her father's house with him one morning. She loved him so much, and he had promised to marry her! He had solemnly promised to marry her, and she had believed him. She was very young, and – and ignorant of what life really is. But he put the marriage off from week to week, and month to month. – She trusted in him all the while. She loved him. – Before her child was born – for she had a child – she implored him for the child's sake to marry her, that the child might have a name, that her sin might not be visited on the child, who was innocent. He refused. After the child was born she left him, taking the child away, and her life was ruined, and her soul ruined, and all that was sweet, and good, and pure in her ruined also. She suffered terribly – she suffers now. She will always suffer. For her there is no joy, no peace, no atonement. She is a woman who drags a chain like a guilty thing. She is a woman who wears a mask, like a thing that is a leper. The fire cannot purify her. The waters cannot quench her anguish. Nothing can heal her! no anodyne can give her sleep! no poppies forgetfulness! She is lost! She is a lost soul! – That is why I call Lord Illingworth a bad man. That is why I don't want my boy to be with him.

GERALD My dear mother, it all sounds very tragic, of course. But I dare say the girl was just as much to blame as Lord Illingworth was. – After all, would a really nice girl, a girl with any nice feelings at all, go away from her home with a man to whom she was not married, and live with him as his wife? No nice girl would.

MRS ARBUTHNOT (*After a pause.*) Gerald, I withdraw all my objections. You are at liberty to go away with Lord Illingworth, when and where you choose.

GERALD Dear mother, I knew you wouldn't stand in my way. You are the best woman God ever made. And, as for Lord Illingworth, I don't believe he is capable of anything infamous or base. I can't believe it of him – I can't.

Jude the Obscure: Thomas Hardy

Jude fell back upon his old complaint – that, intimate as they were, he had never once had from her an honest, candid declaration that she loved or could love him. 'I really fear sometimes that you cannot,' he said, with a dubiousness approaching anger. 'And you are so reticent. I know that women are taught by other women that they must never admit the full truth to a man. But the highest form of affection is based on full sincerity on both sides. Not being men, these women don't know that in looking back on those he has had tender relations with, a man's heart returns closest to her who was the soul of truth in her conduct. The better class of man, even if caught by airy affectations of dodging and parrying, is not retained by them. A Nemesis attends the woman who plays the game of elusiveness too often, in the utter contempt for her that, sooner or later, her old admirers feel; under which they allow her to go unlamented to her grave.'

Sue, who was regarding the distance, had acquired a guilty look; and she suddenly replied in a tragic voice: 'I don't think I like you to-day so well as I did, Jude!'

'Don't you? Why?'

'Oh, well – you are not nice – too sermony. Though I suppose I am so bad and worthless that I deserve the utmost rigour of lecturing!'

'No, you are not bad. You are a dear. But as slippery as an eel when I want to get a confession from you.'

'Oh yes I am bad, and obstinate, and all sorts! It is no use your pretending I am not! People who are good don't want scolding as I do... But now that I have nobody but you, and nobody to defend me, it is *very* hard that I mustn't have my own way in deciding how I'll live with you, and whether I'll be married or no!'

'Sue, my own comrade and sweetheart, I don't want to force you either to marry or to do the other thing – of course I don't! It is too wicked of you to be so pettish! Now we won't say any more about it, and go on just the same as we have done; and during the rest of our walk we'll talk of the meadows only, and the floods, and the prospect of the farmers this coming year.'

Dear Scott, Dearest Zelda: Zelda Fitzgerald

Sweetheart,

Please, please don't be so depressed – We'll be married soon, and then these lonesome nights will be over forever – and until we are, I am loving, loving every tiny minute of the day and night – Maybe you won't understand this, but sometimes when I miss you most, it's hardest to write – and you always know when I make myself – Just the ache of it all – and I *can't* tell you. If we were together, you'd feel how strong it is – you're so sweet when you're melancholy. I love your sad tenderness – when I've hurt you – That's one of the reasons I could never be sorry for our quarrels – and they bothered you so – Those dear, dear little fusses, when I always tried so hard to make you kiss and forget –

Scott – there's nothing in all the world I want but you – and your precious love – All the material things are nothing. I'd just hate to live a sordid, colorless existence – because you'd soon love me less – and less – and I'd do anything – anything – to keep your heart for my own – I don't want to live – I want to love first, and live incidentally. – Why don't you feel that I'm waiting – I'll come to you, Lover, when you're ready – Don't – don't ever think of the things you can't give me – You've trusted me with the dearest heart of all – and it's so damn much more than anybody else in all the world has ever had –

How can you think deliberately of life without me – If you should die – O Darling – darling Scott – It'd be like going blind. I know I would, too. – I'd have no purpose in life – just a pretty – decoration. Don't you think I was made for you? I feel like you had me ordered – and

I was delivered to you – to be worn. I want you to wear me, like a watch-charm or a button hole bouquet – to the world. And then, when we're alone, I want to help – to know that you can't do *anything* without me...

All my heart –
I love you
Zelda

Testament of Youth: Vera Brittain

As Christmas Eve slipped into Christmas Day, I finished tying up the paper bags, and with the Sister filled the men's stockings by the exiguous light of an electric torch. Already I could count, perhaps even on my fingers, the hours that must pass before I should see him. In spite of its tremulous eagerness of anticipation, the night again seemed short; some of the convalescent men wanted to go to early services, and that meant beginning temperatures and pulses at 3 am. As I took them I listened to the rain pounding on the tin roof, and wondered whether, since his leave ran from Christmas Eve, he was already on the sea in that wild, stormy darkness. When the men awoke and reached for their stockings, my whole being glowed with exultant benevolence; I delighted in their pleasure over their childish home-made presents because my own mounting joy made me feel in harmony with all creation.

At eight o'clock, as the passages were lengthy and many of the men were lame, I went along to help them to the communion service in the chapel of the college. It was two or three years since I had been to such a service, but it seemed appropriate that I should be there, for I felt, wrought up as I was to a high pitch of nervous emotion, that I ought to thank whatever God might exist for the supreme gift of Roland and the love that had arisen so swiftly between us. The music of the organ was so sweet, the sight of the wounded men who knelt and stood with such difficulty so moving, the conflict of joy and gratitude, pity and sorrow in my mind so poignant, that tears sprang to my eyes, dimming the chapel walls and the words that encircled them: 'I am the Resurrection and the Life: he that believeth in Me, though he were dead, yet shall he live: and whosoever liveth and believeth in me shall never die.'

Directly after breakfast, sent on my way by exuberant good wishes from Betty and Marjorie and many of the others, I went down to Brighton. All day I waited there for a telephone message or a telegram, sitting drowsily in the lounge of the Grand Hotel, or walking up and down the promenade, watching the grey sea tossing rough with white surf-crested waves, and wondering still what kind of crossing he had had or was having.

When, by ten o'clock at night, no news had come, I concluded that the complications of telegraph and telephone on a combined Sunday and Christmas Day had made communication impossible. So, unable to fight sleep any longer after a night and a day of wakefulness, I went to bed a little disappointed, but still unperturbed. Roland's family, at their Keymer cottage, kept an even longer vigil; they sat up till nearly midnight over their Christmas dinner in the hope that he would join them, and, in their dramatic, impulsive fashion, they drank a toast to the Dead.

The next morning I had just finished dressing, and was putting the final touches to the pastel-blue crêpe-de-Chine blouse, when the expected message came to say that I was wanted on the telephone. Believing that I was at last to hear the voice for which I had waited for twenty-four hours, I dashed joyously into the corridor. But the message was not from Roland but from Clare; it was not to say that he had arrived home that morning, but to tell me that he had died of wounds at a Casualty Clearing Station on December 23rd.

The Collector: John Fowles

I said, excuse me, do you know anything about dogs?

She stopped, surprised. 'Why?' she said.

It's awful, I've just run one over, I said. It dashed out. I don't know what to do with it. It's not dead. I looked into the back, very worried.

'Oh the poor thing,' she said.

She came towards me, to look in. Just as I hoped.

There's no blood, I said, but it can't move.

Then she came round the end of the open back door, and I stood back as if to let her see. She bent forward to peer in, I flashed a look down the road, no one, and then I got her. She didn't make a sound, she seemed so surprised, I got the pad I'd been holding in my pocket right across her mouth and nose, I caught her to me, I could smell the fumes, she struggled like the dickens, but she wasn't strong, smaller even than I'd thought. She made a sort of gurgling. I looked down the road again, I was thinking this is it, she'll fight and I shall have to hurt her or run away. I was ready to bolt for it. And then suddenly she went limp, I was holding her up instead of holding her quiet. I got her half into the van, then I jerked open the other door, got in and pulled her after me, then shut the doors quietly to. I rolled and lifted her on to the bed. She was mine, I felt suddenly very excited, I knew I'd done it. I put the gag on first, then I strapped her down, no hurry, no panic, like I planned. Then I scrambled into the driving-seat. It all took not a minute. I drove up the road, not fast, slow and quiet, and turned to a place I'd noticed on Hampstead Heath. There I got into the back again, and did the tying up properly, with the scarves and everything, so that she wouldn't be hurt, and so she couldn't scream or bang the sides or anything. She was still unconscious, but she was breathing, I could hear her, as if she had catarrh, so I knew she was all right.

My Mother: Jamaica Kincaid

Immediately on wishing my mother dead and seeing the pain it caused her, I was sorry and cried so many tears that all the earth around me was drenched. Standing before my mother, I begged her forgiveness, and I begged so earnestly that she took pity on me, kissing my face and placing my head on her bosom to rest. Placing her arms around me, she drew my head closer and closer to her bosom, until finally I suffocated. I lay on her bosom, breathless, for a time uncountable, until one day, for a reason she has kept to herself, she shook me out and stood me under a tree and I started to breathe again. I cast a sharp glance at her and said to myself, 'So.' Instantly I grew my own bosoms, small mounds at first, leaving a small, soft place between them, where, if ever necessary, I could rest my own head. Between my mother and me now were the tears I had cried, and I gathered up some stones and banked them in so that they formed a small pond. The water in the pond was thick and black and poisonous, so that only unnamable invertebrates could live in it. My mother and I now watched each other carefully, always making sure to shower the other with words and deeds of love and affection.

The Kaleidoscope: Douglas Dunn

To climb these stairs again, bearing a tray,
Might be to find you pillowed with your books,
Your inventories listing gowns and frocks
As if preparing for a holiday.
Or, turning from the landing, I might find
My presence watched through your kaleidoscope,
A symmetry of husbands, each redesigned
In lovely forms of foresight, prayer and hope.
I climb these stairs a dozen times a day
And, by the open door, wait, looking in
At where you died. My hands become a tray
Offering me, my flesh, my soul, my skin.
Grief wrongs us so. I stand, and wait, and cry
For the absurd forgiveness, not knowing why.

One Flesh: Elizabeth Jennings

Lying apart now, each in a separate bed,
He with a book, keeping the light on late,
She like a girl dreaming of childhood,
All men elsewhere – it is as if they wait
Some new event: the book he holds unread,
Her eyes fixed on the shadows overhead.

Tossed up like flotsam from a former passion,
How cool they lie. They hardly ever touch,
Or if they do it is like a confession
Of having little feeling – or too much.
Chastity faces them, a destination
For which their whole lives were a preparation.

Strangely apart, yet strangely close together,
Silence between them like a thread to hold
And not wind in. And time itself's a feather
Touching them gently. Do they know they're old,
These two who are my father and my mother
Whose fire from which I came, has now grown cold?

Clearances 5: Seamus Heaney

The cool that came off sheets just off the line
Made me think the damp must still be in them
But when I took my corners of the linen
And pulled against her, first straight down the hem
And then diagonally, then flapped and shook
The fabric like a sail in a cross-wind,
They made a dried-out undulating thwack.
So we'd stretch and fold and end up hand to hand
For a split second as if nothing had happened
For nothing had that had not always happened
Beforehand, day by day, just touch and go,
Coming close again by holding back
In moves where I was x and she was o
Inscribed in sheets she'd sewn from ripped-out flour
sacks.

First Love: Carol Ann Duffy

Waking, with a dream of first love forming real words,
as close to my lips as lipstick, I speak your name,
after a silence of years, into the pillow, and the power
of your name brings me here to the window, naked,
to say it again to a garden shaking with light.

This was a child's love, and yet I clench my eyes
till the pictures return, unfocused at first, then
almost clear, an old film played at a slow speed.
All day I will glimpse it, in windows of changing sky,
in mirrors, my lover's eyes, wherever you are.

And later a star, long dead, here, seems precisely
the size of a tear. Tonight, a love-letter out of a dream
stammers itself in my heart. Such faithfulness.
You smile in my head on the last evening. Unseen
flowers suddenly pierce and sweeten the air.

Daffodils: Ted Hughes

Remember how we picked the daffodils?
Nobody else remembers, but I remember.
Your daughter came with her armfuls, eager and
   happy,
Helping the harvest. She has forgotten.
She cannot even remember you. And we sold them.
It sounds like sacrilege, but we sold them.
Were we so poor? Old Stoneman, the grocer,
Boss-eyed, his blood-pressure purpling to beetroot
(It was his last chance,
He would die in the same great freeze as you),

He persuaded us. Every Spring
He always bought them, sevenpence a dozen,
'A custom of the house'.

Besides, we still weren't sure we wanted to own
Anything. Mainly we were hungry
To convert everything to profit.
Still nomads – still strangers
To our whole possession. The daffodils
Were incidental gilding of the deeds,
Treasure trove. They simply came,
And they kept on coming.
As if not from the sod but falling from heaven.
Our lives were still a raid on our own good luck.
We knew we'd live forever. We had not learned
What a fleeting glance of the everlasting
Daffodils are. Never identified
The nuptial flight of the rarest ephemera –
Our own days!
We thought they were a windfall.
Never guessed they were a last blessing.
So we sold them. We worked at selling them
As if employed on somebody else's
Flower-farm. You bent at it
In the rain of that April – your last April.
We bent there together, among the soft shrieks
Of their jostled stems, the wet shocks shaken
Of their girlish dance-frocks –
Fresh-opened dragonflies, wet and flimsy,
Opened too early.

We piled their frailty lights on a carpenter's bench,
Distributed leaves among the dozens –
Buckling blade-leaves, limber, groping for air, zinc-
  silvered –

Propped their raw butts in bucket water,
Their oval, meaty butts,
And sold them, sevenpence a bunch –

Wind-wounds, spasms from the dark earth,
With their odourless metals,
A flamy purification of the deep grave's stony cold
As if ice had a breath –

We sold them, to wither.
The crop thickened faster than we could thin it.
Finally, we were overwhelmed
And we lost our wedding-present scissors.

Every March since they have lifted again
Out of the same bulbs, the same
Baby-cries from the thaw,
Ballerinas too early for music, shiverers
In the draughty wings of the year.
On that same groundswell of memory, fluttering
They return to forget you stooping there
Behind the rainy curtains of a dark April,
Snipping their stems.

But somewhere your scissors remember. Wherever they
  are.
Here somewhere, blades wide open,
April by April
Sinking deeper
Through the sod – an anchor, a cross of rust.

Pygmalion's Bride: Carol Ann Duffy

Cold, I was, like snow, like ivory.
I thought *He will not touch me*,
but he did.

He kissed my stone-cool lips.
I lay still
as though I'd died.
He stayed.
He thumbed my marbled eyes.

He spoke –
blunt endearments, what he'd do and how.
His words were terrible.
My ears were sculpture,
stone-deaf, shells.
I heard the sea.
I drowned him out.
I heard him shout.

He brought me presents, polished pebbles,
little bells.
I didn't blink,
was dumb.
He brought me pearls and necklaces and rings.
He called them *girly things*.
He ran his clammy hands along my limbs.
I didn't shrink,
played statue, shtum.

He let his fingers sink into my flesh,
he squeezed, he pressed.
I would not bruise.

He looked for marks,
for purple hearts,
for inky stars, for smudgy clues.
His nails were claws.
I showed no scratch, no scrape, no scar.
He propped me up on pillows,
jawed all night.
My heart was ice, was glass.
His voice was gravel, hoarse.
He talked white black.

So I changed tack,
grew warm, like candle wax,
kissed back,
was soft, was pliable,
began to moan,
got hot, got wild,
arched, coiled, writhed,
begged for his child,
and at the climax
screamed my head off –
all an act.

And haven't seen him since.
Simple as that.

Four Letter Word – New Love Letters: eds Joshua Knelman and Rosalind Porter

I'm not what people would call a 'visual person'. In fact, I'm one of those people who likes the names of flowers so much he can't remember which ones they actually are. You were talking to someone who seemed to be but was not wearing a hat pulled down around his eyes, and as you turned slightly, below your short dark hair one side of your face was no longer shaded but lit pretty clearly by a lamp. I saw one tiny freckle just above the side of your mouth, which turned up just the slightest bit, I wouldn't call it a smile.

I could see it so clearly. All last year I was an artificial lake! Sure I had the occasional requisite live electrical cable dropped into me, but mostly I sat in the sun, full of little nameless waves and cheerful paddle-boats. So many missed chances to blunder. My father told me the problem with us is we are in love with being in love with love. My sister insisted I will just like she and my brother one day eventually learn to follow that feeling of doubt wherever it leads. It's a miracle our people have procreated at all. Yet we persist.

Then it was time to move into the living room. I kept pretending to look for something to write with, trying hard not to watch you laughing and passing a pen back and forth among your friends. When I looked down I saw one of those scraps of paper someone must have dropped. When my turn came I unfolded it and saw someone had written 'I wish I could draw'; without thinking I said 'I see need is no longer only for children' and threw it into the fire.

Many things happened until we met, sort of, finally at the end of the night. You may remember me as tallish by the door. I made a vague motion with my hands like I had either released and immediately begun trying to retrieve something invisible and weightless, or had started to help you with your coat, which I did, clumsily looking down at you from what seemed like an exciting and terrifying altitude. You said your name and turned and did not see me write it on my hand.

Notes

The Miller's Tale: Geoffrey Chaucer (c. 1390)

The Miller's Tale forms part of *The Canterbury Tales*, Chaucer's collection of tales told by a group of characters who are on a pilgrimage to Canterbury. In this tale, Chaucer creates a parody of a tale of courtly romance in response to *The Knight's Tale* which has preceded it. The tale is written in rhyming couplets, allowing Chaucer to explore a variety of complex ideas in a deceptively simple format; as well as broad comedy, he uses subtle humour to challenge attitudes and values.

This extract reveals Nicholas, a scholar, making advances towards Alisoun, the wife of his landlord, the carpenter. We have been told that she is young and very desirable, in contrast to her husband John, who is wealthy but old and ill-educated. His simplicity makes him a prime target for Nicholas's schemes.

1 **eft** again.
so bifel the cas it so happened.
2 **hende** courteous and gentle, but the word also implies Nicholas is skilful in attaining his ends.
3 **yonge wyf** this designation reminds us that Alisoun is a young woman, not long wed to the ageing John the carpenter.
rage and pleye sport and play; these terms suggest wanton behaviour with no lasting commitment.
5 **queynte** sly.
6 **prively he caughte hire by the queynte** this description implies a stealth that we have already seen associated with Nicholas in that he acted *prively* (secretly), but the line clearly has shock value, both in the directness of Nicholas's approach and through the use of the blunt anatomical term *queynte*

(literally meaning 'elegant, pleasing thing' but used as a euphemism for the female genitals).

8 **For deerne love of thee** these words suggest that Nicholas is well versed in the art of secret love affairs, as his words are those of a romantic and conventional lover (*deerne* means secret); but they present us with a striking contrast to the crudity of his actions.

lemman my love.

spille die.

9 **haunchebones** thighs.

12 **sproong as a colt dooth in the trave** Alisoun is described as springing away like a young horse (*colt*). This returns us to an image earlier in the tale of Alisoun as a wild and lively young creature. She is now seen as one who is caught in Nicholas's *trave* (a frame or enclosure used to restrain lively horses while they were shod). It seems that Alisoun has tried to escape only to be trapped by Nicholas's devices.

13 **wryed** twisted.

14–16 Alisoun's first response is to insist that he lets go of her, and that she will cry out for help if he does not behave like a gentleman.

20 **she hir love hym graunted atte laste** after very little persuasion, Alisoun agrees to become his lover; were her protestations merely a flirtatious ruse of playing 'hard to get'?

21 **Seint Thomas of Kent** the very idea that their union should have some religious blessing is against all Christian teachings, but throughout the tale Chaucer uses religious imagery to mock both religious hypocrisy and the behaviour of the protagonists.

25 There is irony to Alisoun's warning here that Nicholas must be cautious, because we know cunning is one of his main characteristics; Nicholas is keen on secrecy and adept at keeping his true motives hidden.

29–30 A scholar would have spent his time wastefully if he didn't know how to get the better of a carpenter. This seems to reveal Nicholas's true intentions; does his passion for Alisoun partly stem from a desire to make a fool of the carpenter?

33 **everideel** all.

34 **thakked hire aboute the lendes** patted her on the thighs. Nicholas is still blunt about the designs he has on Alisoun.
35 **sawtrie** a stringed instrument.
36 The way Nicholas plays his instrument suggests that he is channelling his sexual energy into his vigorous playing, thus suggesting both to Alisoun and to the reader the possibilities of the promised passionate encounter.

The Spanish Tragedy: Thomas Kyd (c. 1590)

Thomas Kyd (1558–1594) is perhaps better known for his alleged involvement in the death of Christopher Marlowe and for his own imprisonment and early death than for his writing. However, in his short career as a playwright Kyd produced *The Spanish Tragedy*, one of the period's most challenging dramas and one that is often considered to have pioneered the form of the revenge tragedy.

As well as considering the nature of revenge, the play explores issues of religion and conflict that were of great concern at the time; Kyd was clearly influenced by the anti-Spanish views that were current when Britain was under threat from Philip II of Spain and his Armada. The plot deals with the idea of love through the framework of revenge, and Kyd gives a critical presentation of the ways in which relationships can be used to control and manipulate instead of to support and enhance people's lives. This extract shows Balthazar's torment: in love with Bellimperia, he hopes to win her but knows that (since he has killed her lover in battle) she loathes him. Rather than celebrating the suitor's passions, Kyd raises the issue of unrequited love in a way that challenges the audience's engagement with the love-sick protagonist.

1 **wilder, and more hard** this description of the object of Balthazar's desires hardly seems complimentary, but refers to

Bellimperia's determination to shun him, suggesting a certain passion in her behaviour. The frustration of the rejected lover is what frames this speech.

2 The list of comparisons adds to the melodrama of his speech but it is interesting to note the images used; the freedom and natural beauty of the first three contrast with the fixed and unmoveable *stony wall* that ends the line. Perhaps Kyd uses these images to suggest Bellimperia's beauty and the passion that cannot be contained.

3 **wherefore** the question beginning with *wherefore* (why) suggests that Balthazar is aware that his frustration is beginning to make him bitter.

5 This rather blunt statement could create sympathy for Balthazar as he realizes that Bellimperia does not find him attractive. It is telling, however, that his first thought is of appearance, not of any emotional or intellectual bond they may have. What might this suggest?

6 **My words are rude** even though he is a man of status, respected by others, Balthazar realizes that his conversation has no charm or subtlety to please Bellimperia.

7 **harsh and ill** these adjectives are striking, as they are a complete contrast to the type of words we would expect a suitor to send to his love; instead they suggest that his anger and frustration are blighting his ability to express his love. Kyd could perhaps be using this idea to satirize the courtly love process.

8 **Pan and Marsyas** Pan is a god in Greek mythology who is half-goat, and Marsyas is a satyr, one of his companions; both are noted for their musical skill. This ironic and rather humorous comparison suggests that Balthazar's skills in writing about love are the opposite of elegant and refined.

9 Continuing the extended list of reasons why Balthazar cannot please, Kyd refers to the final chance a suitor may have by emphasizing that not even tokens of his affection in the form of gifts can win Bellimperia's heart, because they are not costly enough.

10 **worthless** this suggests that Balthazar considers himself to be a failure, consolidated by the reference to the fact that his *labour's lost*. Kyd again plays with the audience's relationship

with Balthazar; do we feel sympathy for him because he seems defeated?

11–20 Kyd uses a repetitive structure for the second part of Balthazar's speech. The lines are a series of couplets with the first line of each starting with *Yet*, posing a possible way in which Bellimperia may fall in love with him; the second line in each pair, beginning with *Ay, but*, shows his lament as he recognizes another reason why she will not be his. Each couplet echoes Balthazar's desperation but also illustrates the things he considers to be the most important characteristics for a successful suitor, which are all rather impersonal.

11–12 This couplet shows Balthazar's belief that his bravery should make Bellimperia love him, if it were not for the fact that, having been captured by Horatio, his current position as prisoner overshadows his success as a soldier.

13–14 In line with courtly practice, Balthazar considers the fact that Bellimperia should agree to be his wife as it will please her father – then he acknowledges that she can reason well and so persuade her father he is not the right suitor.

15–16 Perhaps a little more desperately, Balthazar here considers his friendship with Bellimperia's brother to be a good reason for their match – only to realize she is not interested in pleasing him. The fact that Kyd makes two references to family ties as important factors in relationships highlights the idea that marriage is not simply about two people falling in love. Also interesting to note here is the fact that Kyd is suggesting Bellimperia's capacity for independent thought; she can persuade her father and reject her brother's requests, quite controversial moves for a woman in a patriarchal society.

17–18 Balthazar here believes that the status his wife would enjoy should be a good enough reason to marry. The response to this particular suggestion is that Bellimperia may want someone of higher status. He does not consider the idea that status may not be something Bellimperia would see as significant in choosing a husband.

19–20 Concluding this speech with a rather damning view, this couplet juxtaposes Balthazar's love and frustration. He believes Bellimperia should love him as he is a slave to her beauty and dotes on her, yet his conclusion is that she is not capable of love. Does it seem a little pathetic that he condemns her in such a way merely because she does not return his love, or is Kyd using this to create some sympathy for him?

Edward II: Christopher Marlowe (c. 1592)

Christopher Marlowe was a contemporary of William Shakespeare and was known both for the power of his verse and for the challenging subject matter of his drama. In this passage from near the beginning of the play Gaveston, Edward II's favourite, speaks about his deep knowledge of the king and touches on the sexual nature of their relationship.

1 **wanton poets** the term *wanton* suggests poetry linked to love, passion and lascivious behaviour.

3 This suggests Gaveston's manipulation of the king, and thus implies he may prove to be dangerous to Edward.

5 **masques** balls or gatherings where guests came in disguise (as in *Romeo and Juliet*). The inclusion of this detail is another hint that deceit or self-interest may form part of Gaveston's attachment.

8 **sylvan nymphs** this classical reference is to beautiful mythical creatures that were believed to live in woods.

9 **satyrs** mythical beasts that were half man, half goat and particularly lecherous; another classical image.

10 **antic hay** this reference to pagan activities again reinforces the anarchic nature of Gaveston's relationship with Edward.

11 **Dian's shape** Diana was the goddess of love, but note the reference is to a boy's shape, again suggesting the king's penchant for men.

12 **gilds the water as it glides** this alliterative phrase suggests sensuality; the pace is slowed by the elongated *i* sound in *glides*.

13 **Crownets of pearl** the description suggests luxury, while the word *naked* reinforces the sensual nature of such an encounter.

14 **sportful** playful, frolicking.

15 Another hint of Gaveston's homosexual leanings.

16 **hard by** this can be read as a *double entendre*, meaning 'close by' but also having sexual connotations.

17 **Actaeon** another classical reference from Ovid's *Metamorphoses*; the shepherd Actaeon is changed into a deer (*hart*, 19) because he saw the goddess Diana bathing.
peeping emphasizes the idea of a voyeur enjoying an unintended view of the scene.

20 **die** another sexual image. The French called the moment of sexual climax '*le petit mort*', 'the little death'.

21 This line reiterates Gaveston's claim of deep knowledge about the king's pleasures.

Richard II: William Shakespeare (c. 1595)

Richard II is one of a sequence of plays in which Shakespeare dramatizes the history of England from Plantagenet to early Tudor times. Though some of the most vivid characters in Shakespeare's history plays are people of relatively ordinary birth (notably Falstaff and his companions in the *Henry IV* plays), the action of these plays is built around the struggles over succession to the monarchy, and the triumphs and disasters of the kings who ruled through these times. Shakespeare was intensely interested in kingship and uses these plays to consider the nature and duties of monarchy and the idea of Englishness.

In this speech the dying John of Gaunt, uncle of Richard II, rails against both the attitude and behaviour of his nephew the king. His indignation inspires him to celebrate his love for England; *this scepter'd isle* means so much to him and he feels it is being destroyed by Richard's careless behaviour.

1 **a prophet new inspired** the elderly statesman implies that he has a greater wisdom than mere mortals and can see into the future.

3 **rash fierce blaze of riot** this suggests the impetuous nature of the king. The use of fire imagery also serves to create a sense of the recklessness and destructiveness of Richard's behaviour.

4–5 The balancing of the fire with the water in these lines serves to reinforce the elemental aspects of the king's behaviour.

6–7 These images illustrate the hasty nature of the king; the food imagery also associates his rashness with greed.

8 **insatiate cormorant** this image reinforces the idea of greed: a cormorant is a bird of prey, and it is suggested that its hunger cannot be satisfied. However, this insatiability is seen as a way to self-destruction as it *soon preys upon itself*.

10 **scepter'd isle** the expression involves a synecdoche: the symbol of kingship, the sceptre, comes to represent the whole island.

12 **Eden** Gaunt suggests that England is to be seen as God's own country, like the Paradise created for Adam and Eve.

15 **this little world** this suggests that England is all-embracing, as if it is itself the whole world, though small.

16 Imagery connected with jewellery creates the sense of England's gemlike quality. Through the use of sibilance and monosyllables, the pace is slowed to reinforce the idea of the grandeur of the island.

20–1 Here Shakespeare builds up a list of images that convey the strength of Gaunt's feelings for his country.

24 **Christian service and true chivalry** in linking the religious with the truly honourable, Gaunt celebrates the glories of former kings of England.

25 **sepulchre** a shrine in Judaism where the holy word of God is housed.

27–8 The repetition of *dear* emphasizes the personal emotion in Gaunt's words.

30 **tenement or pelting farm** in mediaeval England land was leased from the lord of the manor; very small areas of land would be leased to peasants.

34 **inky blots and rotten parchment bonds** these suggest the legal documents relating to loans and taxes raised by the king, demonstrating the destructiveness of Richard's financial recklessness and greed, in Gaunt's eyes.

Henry V: William Shakespeare (c. 1598)

Henry V is now perhaps Shakespeare's most famous history play, owing in part to a number of very popular filmed versions (especially the 1944 production, directed by and starring Laurence Olivier, which was released as a piece of wartime propaganda). It is also a play in which Shakespeare is able to explore both the king's role and the workings of patriotism. The character of Henry himself has been carefully constructed over the previous two plays; Shakespeare depicts him as an amoral young man, whose dissolute lifestyle makes him the despair of his father, Henry IV, but who shows his real strengths when he succeeds to the throne. Henry reveals himself as an able leader who inspires an under-strength army to win a momentous victory over the French: and this is the speech, in Act IV scene 3 of the play, with which he spurs his generals to express their love for their country and allegiance to each other by their deeds on the battlefield.

Depending on the staging of the play, this speech can be delivered either in private, to a handful of Henry's leaders, or to the army as a whole. Just before Henry is roused to these words, he has been reviewing the French troops which, at 60,000, outnumber the English soldiers by five to one. His generals gloomily wish each other the best of luck and commend each other to God, clearly doubtful whether they will outlive the day. As Henry enters, the Earl of Westmorland longs for more men, saying, 'O that we now had here/But one ten thousand of those men in England/That do no work today!'. Henry rebukes him, saying their fate is in the hands of God and, he continues, 'The fewer men, the greater share of honour'.

1 **God's peace!** perhaps a surprising choice of words with which to spur men on to battle, this is characteristic of a wide range of oaths used by Shakespeare. Henry reminds his listeners that they are in God's hands and also points them

towards the peace that they will earn – and deserve – as a result of their labours.

honour a crucial concept explored throughout these plays.

4 **host** army.

5 **stomach** in Shakespeare's time temperament was regarded as being clearly linked to the body and its functions. Here a soldier's will to fight is described as being seated in his *stomach*.

7 **crowns for convoy** money for transport costs; a crown (equivalent to 25p today) was not an insignificant sum in Shakespeare's day. Henry is prepared to pay a handsome amount so that any soldier lacking an appetite for the coming battle would have passage back to England.

put into his purse the passive grammatical construction stresses the passiveness of such a man.

9 **fears his fellowship to die with us** is afraid, by being in our company, to die alongside us.

10 **the feast of Crispian** the historical battle of Agincourt occurred on 25 October 1415, which is the feast day of Saints Crispin and Crispinian (or Crispian), twin Roman martyrs. Shakespeare cites these saints (and continues to do so throughout the speech, switching from one to the other in order to fit his metre) to make the occasion seem even more momentous.

21–4 **our names... Salisbury and Gloucester** Henry encourages his generals by referring to them individually. It is a moment of intimacy made more so by his use of a nickname for himself, and the metrical pauses over each name.

26–9 This part of his argument is concluded by Henry's setting the victory (which has not yet been achieved – but his rhetoric has carried his hearers with him and, of course, the audience has the benefit of hindsight) in the context of history to persuade his generals to think of themselves of national heroes.

30 Shakespeare uses a triadic structure as Henry's three phrases bind the English troops together. They are *few* but this means their honour will be greater, and they will be all the more *happy*. Where previously in the speech (see line 8) Henry has perhaps used the 'royal we' (a form available to him speaking as a monarch), here he emphatically uses *we* to encompass all his men.

32 **vile** low born.

33 **gentle his condition** ennoble his status. The use of *gentle* here is a typical Shakespearean conversion of adjective into verb. In Shakespeare's time the word implied high social status more than mildness of character.

34 **gentlemen** the repetition of *gentle* emphasizes that true nobility belongs to the brave rather than to the well-born.

36 **manhoods** a word with broader connotations than it has today, this term incorporates honour as well as physical and sexual prowess.

Much Ado About Nothing: William Shakespeare (c. 1598)

This comedy is noted for its satirical view of courtship customs and its humorous study of love through two contrasting couples. Shakespeare uses the courtship of the two older characters, Beatrice and Benedick, to undermine the idea of courtly behaviour; both go against the unwritten rules of society about how men and women should act with regard to love and marriage. Their witty, intelligent banter at the start of the play makes them attractive to the audience and we see their relationship as one of equals, a rather controversial idea given the gender inequality of the time.

The action of the play, however, centres on the rather fumbled courtship between the dashing soldier Claudio and the genteel young heroine, Hero. At the start of the play Claudio, a well-respected nobleman and brave fighter, reveals his love for Hero, his host's beautiful daughter. Because of a series of misunderstandings and the malicious actions of a few people, the path of their true love is rather bumpy, but, as this is a comedy, the end sees them happily united. In this extract, taken from the opening scene of the play, Claudio discusses his feelings towards Hero with his good friend and confidant Don Pedro. Shakespeare uses this scene to highlight the innocent love Claudio feels but also to make fun of the way in which courtly romances were conducted.

3 **a soldier's eye** Claudio claims he was previously too focused on his role as soldier to be able to look upon Hero like a suitor.

4 **rougher task** note the contrast between love (soft and gentle) and war.

6–7 **war-thoughts… places vacant** now that he is done with soldiering for the time being, Claudio has a space in his mind that can be filled with love.

8 **Come thronging** in contrast to *vacant* in the previous line, this verb creates a sense of vibrancy and seems to suggest that with love will come a feeling of fulfilment.

9–10 What do you think about the emotions presented in these lines? They seem to illustrate Claudio's fear that people will feel he has fallen in love too swiftly, a concern that is developed further later in the extract.

11 Don Pedro's rather fatherly response is interesting as it refers to Claudio's future role as lover. This suggests that the older, wiser Don Pedro feels Claudio is not yet ready to woo Hero and could also indicate that he considers this courtship to be a rite of passage.

13 **cherish it** what impact do you think this phrase has on our response to Don Pedro? The command compounds his role as a father figure offering guidance. It also highlights the idea that he regards love as something to be nurtured and cared for.

14–15 **I will break… thou shalt have her** these lines foreground the nature of courtship and courtly processes, stressing in particular the way in which women became possessions. The fact that Don Pedro boldly states *thou shalt have her* is a clear indication of how women were regarded as a prize for a successful suitor.

17 **minister** Shakespeare plays on the duality of this word; it refers both to the way in which Don Pedro is taking action in response to Claudio's feelings and to the religious role of a minister who would preside over a marriage ceremony.

18 **know love's grief by his complexion** the juxtaposition of *love* and *grief* here points towards the different emotions involved in affairs of the heart – love is seen as something that can be painful and cause sorrow.

19–20 These lines develop the idea seen earlier, that Claudio fears people will judge that he has fallen in love too quickly.

Conventionally there is a need for a courtly procedure to be followed and it is important to be seen to do the right thing, a contrast to the rash spontaneity we may consider romantic.

21 Shakespeare uses a metaphor here for Don Pedro's statement that there is no need to delay love any longer than necessary. This seems practical advice but could also suggest that Hero is expected to be an easy prize.

24 **remedy** this reflects a conventional view of love as a sickness in need of a cure (the possession of the loved one, in this case by marriage).

25–33 Shakespeare introduces an important element of the plot as Don Pedro tells of his plan to disguise himself as Claudio in order to woo Hero and ask her father for her hand in marriage. In the play as a whole it is such meddling (both good-natured and ill-natured) that causes the difficulties in Hero and Claudio's relationship.

Antony & Cleopatra: William Shakespeare (c. 1606)

Although the politics of ancient Rome and Egypt are central to this classic tragedy, what lies at its heart is the power of passionate love. Focusing on the conflict that Octavius Caesar pursues against his rival Marc Antony, together with Antony's lover Cleopatra, Queen of Egypt, the play explores issues of power, trust and honour as well as considering the battle between passion and pragmatism. The opening scene, presented here, is set in Egypt and begins with two Roman soldiers discussing their general's love for the queen. It continues with a glimpse of the relationship between the lovers.

1–2 **dotage... O'erflows** both words suggest that Antony's feelings for Cleopatra are overwhelming, and the use of the term *dotage*, which suggests a foolish fondness, contrasts with the expectations we may have of a Roman general.

4 **plated** clad in armour.

6 **tawny front** dark-skinned forehead (face).
captain's heart Shakespeare juxtaposes the courage of the military leader with his softer emotions.

7–9 **hath burst… bellows and the fan** note the alliteration on the plosive 'b' here. What tone might this suggest? What do you make of the image of the *bellows* (used to fan flames into life) and the *fan*, whose function is to *cool*?

8 **reneges** gives up.

12–13 **The triple pillar… strumpet's fool** the stark contrast between the powerful political figure (a *triple pillar* because he is one of the three rulers of the Roman Empire) and the weak, feeble man controlled by an unworthy lover is striking.

14 Cleopatra's commanding tone here gives an immediate suggestion of her demanding nature.

15 Antony believes true love cannot be measured.

16 **bourn** limit.

18–19 The interruption of the messenger acts as a reminder of Antony's duty and position, yet his response highlights the image of a lover rather than a soldier, the image for which Philo's opening speech prepares us.

19 Antony's curt response expresses his irritation, but he asks for a brief account (*The sum*) of the news.

20 We again sense Cleopatra's controlling nature as she commands Antony to listen to the messenger. What clues can we gather in this extract as to her real feelings here?

21 **Fulvia** Antony's wife, in Rome.

21–4 In the remainder of the speech Cleopatra mocks Antony, suggesting that the message may be from his wife, or from his political rival, the young Caesar. The playful way in which she teases him (here and elsewhere) confirms their close relationship, but she is also highlighting Antony's failings.

29 What do you make of Cleopatra's 'slip of the tongue' in this line?

34 **Let Rome in Tiber melt** the *Tiber* is the river running through Rome. Antony's blatant disregard for his position is quite shocking, but is a tribute to his love for Cleopatra and shows that he does not want to think of anything else.

35–36 **Here is… are clay** the suggestion here is that the privileges brought by ruling *Kingdoms* mean nothing, and that rather than conquering distant lands he is only interested in being here in Egypt with his lover.

40 **weet** recognize.

41 **We stand up peerless** we two cannot be matched.

42 Cleopatra's mention of Antony's wife teases him with her disbelief.

44 **stirred by Cleopatra** Antony responds to his lover's challenging remarks by claiming that he has been awoken by her, implying that all his qualities lay dormant before he met her. Notice how Shakespeare has the lovers completing each other's lines of verse here in quick-fire exchanges, in contrast to their first four lines (14–17), which are like a love poem for two voices.

49 **Hear the ambassadors** despite his attempts to change the subject, Cleopatra still suggests that Antony should hear the message.

50–56 The scene concludes with Antony giving a sense of the sheer vitality and variety of Cleopatra's nature, and of the couple's giddy, exuberant relationship – all the more remarkable for the fact that neither is young.

Sonnet 18: William Shakespeare (1609)

This is arguably Shakespeare's most famous piece of poetry. Written as part of his sonnet collection, which was first published in 1609, the poem is part of the sequence in which Shakespeare writes in praise of a 'fair youth' – possibly, some critics have argued, a young man for whom the writer had an infatuation.

Shakespeare adapts the sonnet structure, writing in iambic pentameter (ten syllables per line in a pattern of unstressed syllables followed by stressed ones), arranged as three quatrains (groups of four lines) each with an *abab* rhyme scheme, and a rhyming couplet at the end.

The conventional, Petrarchan use of the sonnet is to express intense feelings of love, often with the intention of wooing. Here Shakespeare uses a series of metaphors to compare the beauty of the boy to the beauty of nature, highlighting the fragility of such things as the May blossom in comparison with the beauty of the boy, which he can immortalize in his poetry.

1 Opening with the use of the first person and a question engages the reader and establishes a clear voice. Although the use of the first person is common practice in sonnet writing, it is worth noting that the direct address at the opening of the poem obviously establishes a personal tone.

2 **more lovely… more temperate** the repetition of the premodifier *more* here adds emphasis to the boy's beauty, which is considered to outshine that of a summer day. The word *temperate* refers to a perfect temperature: neither too hot nor too cold.

3–8 A series of comparisons highlight the negative or fleeting aspects of nature's beauty.

9–12 What do you notice about the way Shakespeare presents the idea of the constant, unceasing beauty of the boy in this final quatrain? Using direct address makes us feel as if we are party to a private conversation and also helps to highlight the very personal nature of the theme of the poem. By referring to *Death* and by the repetition of *eternal*, Shakespeare suggests that the boy's beauty can outlive all things.

13–14 The rhyming couplet both celebrates the poet's admiration for the young man and highlights the significance of his verse. As long as the sonnet commemorating his beauty is in existence, then the young man can be said to still have life. This is obviously a bold claim to make about one's own writing, but the very fact that you are reading it confirms the thought!

A Valediction: Forbidding Mourning: John Donne (c. 1611)

The Elizabethan poet John Donne (1572–1631) is often considered the greatest of the Metaphysical poets as his work ranges over many different issues and ideas. His most engaging works present the trials of love and explore the many ways in which love affects the human condition. It is thought that in this poem Donne is addressing his wife before he set outs on a journey to the Continent that will separate them for some time. A *Valediction* is a poem of farewell. We can see that the poet is concerned with absence but believes that it will be a worthwhile and necessary experience. The title implies a command, and both it and the poem itself demand that, though the two of them may be sad while they are apart, they must not wallow in melancholy.

1–2 Donne establishes an image of those who must part as *souls*. He seems to suggest that their parting is a virtuous thing, or at least an opportunity to act virtuously. The extended simile introduced here suggests that their parting is like the quiet death of *virtuous men* as, though it is sad, it should also be celebrated as they will be rewarded in heaven.

2 **whisper to their souls** notice the use of the soft-sounding verb *whisper*, suggesting secretiveness, as well as the reference to *souls*. Both suggest that the situation is a serious one and brings sorrow.

3–4 Donne creates the sense that the departure may have two different reactions: there will be those who accept the journey (*The breath goes now*) and those who fight to delay the inevitable (*some say, no*). They are all *sad friends*, suggesting the pain caused regardless of one's reaction to the separation.

5 **So let us melt** what impact does the use of *melt* have here? The verb has romantic connotations as it may make us think of the heart melting. The use of the pronoun *us* creates an image of unity.

make no noise this image conjures up the idea of a secret lovers' meeting. In the extended simile of the dying men, Donne is suggesting that any complaints or expressions of sadness would disturb the peace of the passing.

6 **tear-floods, nor sigh-tempests** the weather imagery strikingly suggests that he understands the power of such emotions, but they are destructive as they will overpower the happiness of love that should be the focus for them in difficult times when apart.

7 **'Twere profanation** it would be sacrilege, blasphemy. This term creates a sense of the lovers' relationship as something holy, a higher, purer one than that of others.

8 **the laity** people who are involved in a church or religion but not ordained in any official capacity. Again Donne implies that the lovers' relationship is something uniquely pure.

9 **Moving of th' earth** disasters such as earthquakes. Donne is drawing an analogy with a parting between lovers who are controlled by earthly, physical desires.

harms and fears the result of an earthquake, and also of the parting of those who are led by their physical desires.

11 **trepidation of the spheres** in Donne's time it was believed that the universe was made up of a series of *spheres*, with the earth at their centre, whose movement and vibration (*trepidation*) produced heavenly music that ordinary humans had lost the power to hear. It is the movement that causes this celestial music, so it is much more powerful than an earthquake but entirely beneficial (*innocent*). The analogy is to the more spiritual and intellectual love he and his wife share (it is like the *spheres* rather than the *earth*).

13 **Dull** commonplace.

sublunary literally 'situated under the moon'. In mediaeval astronomy, everything below the moon shared in the fall of humankind – even the earth itself, though God's creation, demonstrated its imperfection through natural disasters (*Moving of th' earth*). Here again the poet asserts that those who experience love merely through physical desires occupy a status below his and his wife's.

14 **Whose soul is sense** ordinary lovers miss each other because the physical (*sense*) is all there is to their relationship. Note the use of alliteration and sibilance here.

14–15 **cannot admit/Absence** those who live only for the pleasures of the flesh will suffer if separated, as there is no other means for them to connect with their lovers.

18 **our selves know not what it is** their bond is so pure that it is difficult for even them to grasp it.

19 **Inter-assured** what meanings do you find in this striking word?

21–4 This stanza compares the relationship to *gold*, the purest and most precious substance. In a complex simile typical of the Metaphysical style, the poet explains that his absence (which, he reminds his wife in a quick parenthesis, is something that *must* happen) rather than bringing about a *breach* or separation between the two of them, will actually enhance their closeness, and result in an *expansion* of their intimacy; just as *gold* becomes *refined* (line 17) when it is *to aery thinness beat* (thus occupying a larger area).

25–8 This stanza introduces perhaps Donne's most famous extended simile. Conceding that his and his wife's *souls* may indeed be *two* rather than one, Donne contends that they are only two in the sense that they are like two feet of the same mathematical compass. The *fixed foot* (here the one belonging to *Thy soul*) has to stay firm so that the other can roam freely. However, it does *move... if th'other do*, as the next stanza explains.

29–32 The further one foot extends, the more the other, while still fixed *in the centre, leans, and hearkens after it*, becoming *erect* (here implying confidence, but perhaps also with a sexual meaning) as the compass narrows and the two feet are brought together again.

33–6 The poet concludes on a flattering note. Casting himself as *th' other foot*, the one that must *obliquely run*, he maintains that it is only his wife's *firmness* that makes his *circle* accurate or perfect (*just*). A *circle* was an important symbol of wholeness and purity in Elizabethan times. Continuing the extended simile to conclude his argument, his journey must *end, where I begun* – as a circle does.

On My First Daughter: Ben Jonson (1616)

Ben Jonson, a contemporary of Shakespeare, wrote both plays and poems. He had a varied career including being a soldier, and was once imprisoned on a murder charge, having killed an opponent in a duel. He escaped the death penalty as a result of his connections with the clergy. His plays tend to be satiric in nature but this poem offers us a different view of Jonson as we see him mourning a loss and asserting his belief in God. The poem, published in 1616, was written on the loss of his daughter Mary, who died aged only six months in 1593.

1 **ruth** generally means 'mercy', but here 'sorrow' seems more fitting.

3–4 Jonson insists in this rhyming couplet that the grief he feels is lessened by the knowledge that the child has been taken by God, as she was God's gift and therefore he is at liberty to reclaim her.

6 The fact that the child died so young is also presented in a positive light, as the parents can be sure she has died untainted by sin.

7–9 The child has the same name as *heaven's queen*, the Virgin Mary, the mother of Christ, and the poet asserts that, because of the child's innocent status, the Virgin will herself care for her soul.

10 **that severed** the soul that has parted from the body.

11 **the fleshly birth** the poet suggests that, as a result of being in the Virgin's care, the child has in fact undergone a rebirth, superior to the *fleshly* one.

'Tis Pity She's a Whore: John Ford (1633)

John Ford (1586–1640) is often considered to be the last of the great Renaissance dramatists. *'Tis Pity She's a Whore* is his most famous work, bringing him much critical acclaim. Based on the story of the incestuous relationship between Annabella and her brother Giovanni, it incorporates many features of a Jacobean tragedy, though it was written when Charles I was on the throne.

The play is noted for its dark, macabre tone and celebrated for the strikingly dramatic and bloody conclusion, but its real strength lies in its challenging presentation of the couple. Ford presents the lovers in a compassionate manner and at times seems keen to engage the audience's sympathies even though their relationship, in either his own society or modern ones, would be considered illegal and unhealthy. This sympathy often stems from comparisons with other characters in the play as it seems that nobody is free from guilt and those we would expect to be most virtuous (religious figures, for example) are shown to be the most corrupt. In this extract, the function of which is to first introduce the relationship between the two lovers, we are led to empathize with their plight as they wrestle with their illicit emotions.

1 **Lost, I am lost** there is a sense of despair here and the repetition makes the line like a lament. This immediately engages the audience and creates sympathy for the character. **my fates have doomed my death** the repetition of the personal pronoun indicates that Giovanni acknowledges some responsibility as well as blaming the *fates*, but the vocabulary is dark, suggesting the inevitability of tragic consequences for the relationship.

2–3 **The more… I hope** the cyclical nature of these lines reflects Giovanni's confusion and distress. The contrast between *strive* and *love*, coupled with the reference to a loss of *hope*, is also striking, as it is usually thought that love should by contrast bring pleasure and optimism. This illustrates the doomed nature of the relationship and shows how aware he is of his and his sister's likely fate. Again, Ford is creating sympathy for the lovesick Giovanni.

3 **I see my ruin, certain** Giovanni is conscious of his destiny. The audience will be expecting a dark conclusion to the tragedy.

5 **incurable and restless wounds** the use of phrases associated with illness suggests that his passion is something natural and uncontrollable.

6 **in vain** the phrase is again associated with hopelessness.

7 Beginning the line with O adds to the sense that this is a soliloquy of lament.

8 Ford establishes an extended metaphor here, comparing the relationship with religious images. This serves two purposes: first, it makes the audience aware that Giovanni considers the

relationship to be something beautiful and worthy of admiration; second, it reminds us of the fact that the lovers will be punished not only on earth but by God too, a theme central to the play as a whole.

9 **wearied Heaven with prayers** the verb *wearied* echoes the frustration that has been established. The fact that Giovanni is turning to God again reflects the religious theme of the play and could create sympathy.

10 **The spring of my continual tears** how might this natural image affect the audience's view of Giovanni?

10–11 **starved/My veins with daily fasts** phrases associated with hunger suggest his sexual appetite, and also link to the image of the *spring* earlier, suggesting his love is natural and uncontrollable.

13–14 **old men's… unsteady youth** the juxtaposition of young and old here reminds us of Giovanni's impulsive youthfulness, and the premodifier *unsteady* adds to this. The contrast also illustrates the young love being condemned by the elders and old rules.

16 **my fate** this second reference to fate not only suggests that it is destiny that is driving the lovers together but argues that Giovanni's feelings are not driven solely by his sexual desires (*lust*).

18 **I'll tell her that I love her** this stark and direct statement creates a sense of anticipation as the audience await his revelation. How does this impact on our view of the lovers?

19 **the price of that attempt** the reference to monetary value reminds us of the price of love.

20 **O me! She comes** the exclamation reflects Giovanni's excitement but also fear of what he is about to do.
Brother this is a timely reminder for the audience of the blood relationship between the two.

20–2 **If such… my tongue** this aside illustrates Giovanni's anxiety but also creates a sense of anticipation.

24–5 The simple exchange emphasizes their relationship as that of brother and sister as well as, once again, developing the relationship between the couple and the audience.

25–6 **methinks you are not well** again referring to their love as a sickness, and suggesting that his suffering is physical as well as emotional.

34–6 This can be seen as an uncomplicated, beautiful meeting of brother and sister, walking hand in hand. The audience is therefore able to develop a bond with them prior to the revelation of their incest later in the play.

Deo Salvatori: Thomas Fettiplace (1659)

This seventeenth-century verse, by a little-known writer who died in 1670, reflects the religious views of the time. Taken from *The Sinner's Tears, in Meditations and Prayers*, it is a simple prayer to God, describing the act of prayer and sacrifice through dedication to religious belief, and asking for help in making thoughts pure in order to be able to see the grace of God. The verse uses a simple *aabb* rhyme scheme.

5 **sovereign balm** the noun phrase refers to the power of God as the *sovereign* to heal and cure.
vouchsafe grant.
7 **Inlighten** enlighten, give insight and inspiration.

The Clod and the Pebble: William Blake (1794)

William Blake was born in London in 1757 and lived for most of his life there. Blake's father apprenticed his visionary and resolutely individual son to an engraver, and Blake earned a living from this craft, often producing pictures to illustrate the work of others, although his ambition was to publish his own illustrated poems and sketches.

In 1789 Blake printed the first edition of his *Songs of Innocence*, adding *Songs of Experience* in 1794, from which *The Clod and the Pebble* is taken, and issuing both series bound together. The poems were characterized by profound ideas expressed in deceptively simple ways, their imagery drawn from nature and the Bible and their versification exploiting the forms of nursery rhymes and hymns.

Songs of Innocence and of Experience, like all Blake's works, conveys a highly individual philosophical and religious outlook. Blake held radical views on matters such as social justice and sexual freedom, and had nothing but contempt for institutions such as the established Church and the monarchy, distrusting the cold rationalism which dictated their actions and censuring them for condoning the existence of oppression and poverty. Experiencing visions from an early age, Blake saw himself as a prophet and his writings increasingly served a prophetic function. One of his key convictions was that opposites, such as good versus bad, should coexist in tension; as he put it in his 1793 work *The Marriage of Heaven and Hell*, 'without contraries is no progression'.

While the *Songs of Innocence* portray a fresh, idealistic, sometimes nostalgic outlook on life and feature a God of love, the *Songs of Experience* tend to be cynical and bitter, depicting a world where God is, at best, to be feared. Neither perspective represents a 'right' view: both have to be held together. It seems that Blake even believed that evil was as essential as good.

In *The Clod and the Pebble*, Blake typically takes two views of love and expresses them via two different mouthpieces. What is clear is that both kinds of love – both the purely altruistic and the chillingly cynical – exist in the world; and, as in this poem, both call themselves love. One possible reading argues that the Pebble's perception of love, while selfish, is at least realistic. Blake may be implying that the motives that underlie the Clod's type of love are less innocent than they seem.

Blake chooses tetrameters and a simple *abab* rhyme scheme, like a hymn, for this poem. He also uses the characteristic vocabulary and grammar of hymns.

1 **Love seeketh** the Clod's ideas are made more accessible by

the personification of *Love*, which gives the sense not of an abstraction but of a person making decisions on how to act. The *–th* verb suffixes were becoming archaic in formal writing by Blake's time, but recall the vocabulary of hymns.

1–3 These lines are a summary of I Corinthians 13 – but Blake stresses the utter selflessness of this sort of love by showing us three elements of it.

4 The speaker highlights the strength of this love. Conventional Christianity in Blake's time understood despair to be the worst of sins and the most desperate of conditions, since it signified a world completely without the love of God.

5–7 Only in the second stanza does Blake reveal the names and personalities of his speakers. The images of the Clod and the Pebble have given rise to numerous interpretations by scholars. The Clod represents the traditional Christian virtue of 'turning the other cheek'. Its passiveness is emphasized by Blake's positioning of *Trodden* at the beginning of line 6. The picture that accompanies this poem features a range of solid-looking animals firmly treading down the earth. Blake is perhaps implying that the Clod is too willing to be at the mercy of others or to be pummelled into a shape that others require. On the other hand, *Clay* is an image much used in the Bible where God is portrayed as a potter fashioning believers into better people. The hardness of the Pebble carries connotations of selfishness but also confidence and endurance. That the Pebble represents experience rather than innocence is suggested by the epithet *of the brook*: in Blake's work, water often symbolizes materialism.

8 The Pebble's self-assurance is also expressed by Blake's use of *Warbled* to convey the cheerfulness and attractiveness of the stone's song. The *metres* are rhythmic lines, and he describes the rhythms as *meet* (appropriate), although it is worth noting that irony is often important in the *Songs of Experience*.

9 Blake invites us to compare the two forms of love by paralleling this line closely with line 1.

10 Blake explores the possessive side of love in a number of poems in *Songs of Experience*.

11 Again Blake uses vocabulary very similar to the words of the first stanza to pinpoint the difference between the two views of

love. He also recalls the statement in I Corinthians 13:6 that love 'rejoiceth not in iniquity', to show how unlike conventional Christian charity the Pebble's love is.

12 As in the first stanza, the choice of *builds* implies a conscious crafting. Blake parallels *despair* in the first stanza with *despite* here to reinforce the maliciousness of the Pebble. However, it would be too simplistic to read this final stanza as a censure of this type of love. In other works, Blake often praises Hell as a place where spontaneity and energy can have free rein.

Lines composed while climbing the left ascent of Brockley Coomb: S.T. Coleridge (1795)

One of the leading poets of the Romantic movement, Samuel Taylor Coleridge (1772–1834) is perhaps best known for his collaboration with William Wordsworth to produce *Lyrical Ballads*. He believed that poetry should be a reflection of the writer's relationship with the natural world and should be constructed from the passions of the soul. This poem encapsulates the joy the poet experiences when surrounded by nature, and shows his love for the countryside. The poem is essentially about engaging with one's emotions and opening oneself to what the natural world can offer, as Coleridge describes the beautiful images that surround and inspire him. It ends, however, with a reflection of the speaker's love for a human being.

2 **sweet songsters** the sibilance here echoes the sound of the birds.

3 **wild-wood** the alliteration again creates a sensory experience and reflects the speaker's enjoyment of the landscape.

4 **unvarying Cuckoo soothes** the adjective *unvarying* creates a sense of the constant presence of nature, and the verb *soothes* tells us of the poet's love for it.

6 **browse** graze.

7 **forc'd fissures of the naked rock** the fricative sounds here echo the jagged nature of the rocks being described, and add to the sense of awe at the natural beauty.

8 **The Yew tree bursts!** this exclamation and the use of the lively verb *bursts* add to the engagement with the powerful landscape.

10 **mossy seats** the surroundings, though rugged, are welcoming as the stones accommodate him, becoming seats where he can *rest*.

12 **Ah! what a luxury of landscape** the exclamative tone, the use of the adjective *luxury* and the alliteration all emphasize the passion of the response.

14 **prospect-bounding Sea!** again the exclamation echoes the poet's excitement and delight at the sights. Coleridge also uses the sea as a metaphor for hopes of the future. Being surrounded by such beauty he cannot help but feel inspired.

15 Despite being surrounded by the landscape he clearly loves, the speaker feels melancholy at having nobody with whom to share it.

16 Still mourning the death of his love, the poet remains captivated by the *Enchanting* scene, but sad that the experience cannot be shared.

The First Tooth: Mary Lamb (1809)

With her brother Charles, Mary Lamb (1764–1847) wrote a series of texts for children. Their most famous work, *Tales from Shakespeare*, is still in print today. They also wrote poetry that was, although very simple in style, intensely emotional and often focused on important experiences from their childhood. In this verse, Lamb illustrates the jealousy often seen in sibling rivalry and uses a conversational style to present the relationship between sister and brother.

1 **busy joy** the description here establishes a sense of the excitement the new tooth has created. Lamb constructs an

image of the home that is instantly full of happiness, yet the persona seems a lone voice, separate from this.

2 **the infant boy** there is a humorously derogatory tone here as the persona fails to give the baby a name, and instead uses a rather distant, universal reference.

3 **tiny tooth** what impact does the sound patterning have here? The alliterative phrase seems quite critical and harsh, with emphasis on the insignificant size of the tooth, but it also points up the fact that the vocabulary and phrasing are innocently child-like.

4 The *double row* contrasts with the *tiny tooth* of the speaker's brother, and the use of the personal pronoun at the start of the line foregrounds the divide between the two siblings.

5 **All as… all as** the repetition again serves to highlight the contrast between the two and shows that the persona feels she needs to compete with her brother for attention.

7–10 Here the speaker uses a similar structure in comparing the brother's development to her own, this time focusing on his speech. There is charm in the presentation of the character offering a simple, child-like view of her brother's development; the implicit criticism creates humour.

11–14 Again Lamb uses contrasts to illustrate the jealousy of the sister as she compares her brother's infant movements with her *best dancing*.

15–16 This first part of the brother's reply directly addresses the sibling and, though there seems to be a humorous tone, it issues a clear warning. What do you make of the voice Lamb creates for the brother?

17 **smallest seed should be** the sibilance and assonance here emphasize the warning.

17–20 Lamb uses an extended metaphor to warn of jealousy by comparing the initial thoughts to a *seed* that may grow and produce painful consequences.

21 There is a clear sense of the brother's affection for his sister here.

23–30 Lamb repeats the three stages of child development referred to in the first section of the poem.

27 **Phoenix** a mythical bird which, having been consumed by fire, was reborn from the ashes. Lamb uses the simile to

humorously emphasize the way the first tooth is considered a great milestone.

31 **encomiums** formal expressions of praise (a humorous exaggeration).

34 Lamb ends the poem with an important reference to the significance of *praise*, which is as nourishing for children as the *milk* needed for healthy growth.

The Eve of St Agnes: John Keats (1819)

This is an extract from a long poem by John Keats (1795–1821), who is associated with the latter part of the Romantic movement. His work is characterized by rich, sensual language and vivid description. In this passage the young Porphyro has gained access to Madeline's bedroom. It is St Agnes's Eve, and she has become entranced by the superstition that on this particular night one can dream of one's future lover. As in the Romeo and Juliet story, the two families of the young people are feuding and therefore they have little chance of their families' approval of their relationship. In this passage Porphyro sees Madeline asleep and is overwhelmed by her beauty and vulnerability.

1 **azure-lidded** this compound adjective uses the subtlety of the delicate blue colour, with its connotations of the sky or heavens, to create an image of purity and innocence in the sleeping Madeline.

2 **blanchèd linen** the starched white of the bed linen again emphasizes the virginal nature of the young girl.

4–5 The listing of these exotic fruits and the description of the jellies creates a sensuous atmosphere in direct contrast to the rather sterile purity of Madeline's bed.

7 **Manna** a sweet substance produced by the tamarisk tree.

argosy merchant ship.

8 **Fez** probably Keats is referring to a place in the eastern Mediterranean, most likely Turkey.

9 **silken Samarkand to cedared Lebanon** again places in the East; the mention of the products for which they are famed gives a sense of the exotic and luxurious.

10–11 **glowing hand/On golden dishes** notice how warmth and light are associated with Porphyro.

12–14 **sumptuous... chilly room** the contrast between the opulence of the dishes and the silence and chill of the night mirrors the difference in the emotional temperature of Madeline and Porphyro at this point.

16 **eremite** a religious hermit. The biblical imagery of this line allows Keats to present Porphyro's intrusion as a kind of spiritual awakening.

18 **my soul doth ache** in the manner of all courtly lovers, Porphyro is suffering because his attentions are at this point unrequited. His pain is emotional and spiritual, so his intrusion into the young woman's chamber is presented as having a religious purity.

19 **warm, unnervèd** these words, in contrast to the previous line, emphasize the sensual nature of the encounter.

20 **Sank in her pillow** the description reveals the very close proximity between Porphyro and the sleeping girl.

21 **'twas a midnight charm** Keats creates a fairytale world in which the girl sleeps in an unbroken spell.

22–4 In these lines Keats creates a contrast between the warmth associated with passion and the cold linked to virginal purity. There is a richness and opulence in the description that is balanced by the image of the *iced stream*.

27 **woofèd** woven. The idea of the spell is developed again through the use of archaic language, as Porphyro too appears to be woven into the charm in her dreaming state.

29 The juxtaposition of *Tumultuous* and *tenderest* conjures up the balance explored in the poem between passion and pure love.

31 **'La belle dame sans mercy'** literally translated as 'the beautiful woman who shows no mercy', this phrase echoes the plight of other courtly lovers who have complained through the ages of unrequited love. Keats also wrote a poem with this title.

33–4 **soft moan... panted quick** the description here appears to mimic sexual arousal. Note the use of short, staccato phrases that serve to build up Porphyro's anticipation.

35 **blue affrayèd eyes** her eyes reflect Madeline's innocence and virginal quality.

36 **pale as smooth-sculptured stone** this description portrays Porphyro as something of a victim of Madeline's beauty as he is metaphorically turned to stone.

39–42 Here Keats illustrates one of the key issues that he explores in much of his poetry, the unrelenting harshness of reality in contrast to the world of the imagination. Madeline's reaction to waking from her dream of Porphyro to find the real young man in her bedchamber is one of fear and shock; for her, the world has suddenly become both threatening and disappointing.

44–5 Keats now portrays Porphyro, whose very name suggests passion and desire, as saintlike. Once again the idea is of the courtly lover being overwhelmed by the presence of the beautiful, unobtainable woman.

49 In her dream, she saw Porphyro in religious terms, as *spiritual* and *clear*.

50 The reality appears to be quite different: the man she encounters in her bedchamber has changed from the ideal of her dream and is *pallid* (drained of blood, linking back to the image of Porphyro as a *stone*), *chill, and drear*.

54 Here Madeline seems to fear that Porphyro is sick, and Keats presents us with her sense of desperation; the relationship is one of female dependency and vulnerability.

55 Keats seems to offer an excuse for Porphyro's behaviour here, in that his passions exceed those of *mortal man* and in consequence are not, presumably, subject to the same moral codes.

57–8 The sexual imagery here is counterbalanced by the calm, restful blue of heaven. The colour imagery contrasts passion and desire with purity.

59–61 **Into her dream... Solution sweet** the moment of sexual union is created through a fusion of colour imagery, as the *rose* of Porphyro blends with the *violet* of Madeline and he is *melted* into her dream.

61–3 **Meantime the frost-wind... St Agnes' moon hath set** the extract concludes with a reminder of the cold and uncompromising world outside Madeline's bedchamber; once again Keats uses concrete images to illustrate the contrast between the world of passion and desire and what the future may hold for two star-crossed lovers.

Letter to Fanny Brawne: John Keats (1820)

This extract is from one of a series of letters written between 1819 and 1820 addressed to Keats's neighbour, Fanny Brawne, who eventually became his fiancée just before his death from tuberculosis. Though Keats is of course best known for his work as a poet, these letters give us a sense of his skill as a prose writer. Perhaps most tellingly, they allow us a glimpse of the passionate nature that inspired his work and the constant state of emotional turmoil in which he lived.

The letters are sometimes touchingly sentimental and romantic, but this one interestingly presents his mistrust of Fanny and her 'inappropriate' behaviour. This insight into the jealousy and despair love can bring makes an interesting contrast to what we would usually expect in a love letter. He clearly wishes to provoke a response and to control Fanny's behaviour. A modern audience may feel this is emotional blackmail, but it is difficult not to have some sympathy for the tortured lover.

2 **occupied with nothing but you** this is in line with the type of expression we would expect to see in a love letter, as it suggests he is missing her while they are apart. The sentiment reminds us of the obsession often associated with love, but in the context of the whole letter it is something rather different as Keats's inability to think of anything or anyone else is driven by jealousy.

3–4 **tormented day and night** again this echoes the kind of vocabulary we would perhaps expect to see in a love letter; these words create the sense that the writer is haunted by the sadness of separation. The verb *tormented* is particularly evocative of the pain and frustrations of love.

5 **recover** referring to the need to *recover* may make us think of love as an illness, an image we have seen elsewhere in literature dealing with the theme; but Keats was also seriously ill with tuberculosis.

9 **agonies** consider why Keats once again describes his sufferings with a word associated with both physical and emotional pain.

10 **sudden and expert** this description of how he will question her mother about her supposed inappropriate behaviour is striking as the two words contrast and therefore illustrate his dilemma. *Sudden* suggests the urgency his jealousy will cause, whereas *expert* creates the image of someone who is in control. Keats presents the range of emotions he is feeling.

12–13 **literally worn to death** the premodifier *literally* makes this phrase quite melodramatic, but do you find the sentiment touching nonetheless?

15 **deathful** this word links with the previous images of illness and death. What impact might this have on the presentation of his love?

16–17 **the habit of flirting with Brown** in a direct and accusatory tone, Keats makes it clear that he is referring to repeated behaviour; it is a *habit*. The word *flirting* bluntly makes his complaints clear, but this can also be seen as something quite frivolous, in contrast to the pain it causes.

18 **pang** sudden feeling of emotional distress.

19–20 **doing me to death by inches** the blame is very much placed on the woman here. She is, by her actions, slowly killing him.

21–3 Why does Keats use the repetition of *though* here?

24 **I will never** a blunt and direct retort, this shows Keats's determination not to waver in his demands.

26–7 **I *will* resent... made a football** how does this metaphor affect the way we judge the writer?

27 **You will call this madness** as with many people driven by jealousy, Keats acknowledges the fact that others will not understand. But by using the personal pronoun *you* throughout this particular section (he continues through to line 40) he is maintaining his rather accusatory tone.

30–1 **You are to me an object intensely desireable** the use of *object* here sounds rather derogatory to a modern reader, but the sentiment is clear and the use of the adverb *intensely* emphasizes his passionate obsession.

31–2 **the air I breathe… is unhealthy** though the image is hardly a beautiful one, the notion that Keats cannot live without Fanny is striking here. Notice again the reference to ill health.

33 **no – you can wait –** once again the hesitations created through the use of the dashes echo Keats's desperation and confusion. There is a sense that the poet understands that what he is saying may sound cruel, but acknowledging that she does not feel as strongly towards him as he does towards her is painful.

34–5 **Any party… has been enough** the ideas here link with the reference earlier to Fanny's *flirting*, as they seem to suggest that she is frivolous and this makes her uncaring. The repetition of *any* emphasizes the fact that she does not care how she fills her day, which seems to be adding to his frustrations.

35–6 **How have… smil'd with?** using a pair of questions, Keats emphasizes his frustrations but also maintains his accusations.

36–7 **All this may seem savage in me** we can have sympathy for Keats here as he acknowledges the harshness of his own tone, though the modal *may* and the use of *seem* suggests that he believes his *savage* actions can be justified.

40 **Keats has… in Loneliness** the capitalization of *Loneliness* elevates it to a place where Keats clearly feels he has resided for a long time. Notice also the reference to himself in the third person.

40–1 **For myself I have been a Martyr** the noun *Martyr* is a powerful term to use in this context. Often associated with religious sacrifice and suffering, it is usually used in pious contexts. To consider himself to have suffered so much may seem melodramatic to the reader.

44–5 **Do not write… have seen** still maintaining the melodrama, Keats's demand here shows clearly his lack of trust for her, and we can sense the guilt he wishes to instil in her. What does this suggest about his feelings towards her?

47–9 **I do not want… I cannot live** going back to the images of pain and suffering used at the start of the letter, these phrases add a new level of drama to his plight.

50 **not only you but *chaste you; virtuous you*** the use of italics emphasizes the request and highlights the standard he expects from her. The use of *chaste* is particularly striking, as it suggests both moral and sexual purity.

50–1 **The Sun rises and sets, the day passes** what do you think Keats's main aim is here? There is a rather dreary tone and he could perhaps be emphasizing the perpetual nature of his misery.

53–4 **the quantity of… in a day** there is a real sense of melodrama again here. Does he rather labour his point in an attempt to ensure that Fanny feels guilty at having caused him so much pain?

54 **Love is not a plaything** there is some irony in this statement as it could be argued that Keats has been playing with his emotions throughout the letter.

55–6 **crystal conscience** he is reiterating the fact that she must be perfectly free from guilt.

56 **than –** the dash here suggests that Keats is unable to voice the fears he has.

Jane Eyre: Charlotte Brontë (1847)

The eldest of the three famous Brontë sisters, Charlotte (1816–1855) is best known for this novel, which tracks the development of the rather unconventional heroine of the title. The story is essentially a journey of self-discovery and centres on Jane as she moves from adolescence into adulthood. The relationship between Jane and her employer, Edward Rochester, is the most striking part of the story. This extract, taken from the last chapter, reflects some of Brontë's rather unconventional ideas about marriage. At a time when women were expected to take a subservient position within a household, the notion that Rochester and Jane are equals by the end of the novel was a rather radical idea. The extract explores the idea of true love and

Brontë presents what seems to be an idealized image of what marriage should be like.

1–4 Brontë uses this opening section to establish a summative tone and to draw attention to the fact that her narrator is to offer her own opinions on the topic of her marriage.

6 **for and with** this is the first indication of unity and equality.

7–8 **supremely blest... language can express** the repetition of *blest* emphasizes the extreme emotion being presented, and the ironic reference to her emotions being beyond what can appear on a page makes the reader understand that the love is unbounded.

8–9 **I am my husband's life as fully as he is mine** this offers a liberating image of equality and a celebration of the way in which two people can give themselves to each other wholeheartedly.

10–11 **bone of his bone and flesh of his flesh** what impression do the religious overtones of this phrase (see Genesis 2:23) give you about Jane's perception of the relationship?

11–12 **I know no weariness... none of mine** the balance between the two is illustrated here through the use of punctuation. The line pivots around the colon, and it is interesting that the female perspective is placed first, showing the narrator's status – no longer does the female have to be submissive.

13–14 **the pulsation... separate bosoms** the use of the singular for *heart* and plural for *bosoms* presents the idea that though they share a connection through their love (their one *heart*), Jane and Rochester are still separate entities (with two *bosoms*) and as such still remain individual. This leaves us with the sense that their love unites but does not consume them. What does this tell us of Brontë's view of marriage?

14–15 **we are ever together** the adverb *ever* refers to the idea of Jane's and Rochester's eternal love.

15–16 **To be together... as in solitude** again Brontë uses terms that emphasize the freedom within their relationship.

19–20 **we are precisely... the result** the idea that being perfectly suited is vital to a successful relationship shows that Brontë believes love must be based on a meeting of minds to be successful. Ending the paragraph with the reference to *concord* (harmony) stresses the beauty of their relationship.

21 **Mr Rochester continued blind** much has been made of the fact that Brontë only reunites the lovers in the novel when Rochester has been injured and is in need of help, so Jane can become his physical as well as intellectual equal.

25–6 **He saw... books through me** the idea that Jane is the one who provides both emotional and intellectual stimulus for Rochester elevates her status; arguably she becomes more powerful than he is.

31 **Never did I weary** the repetition of this phrase from lines 26–7 emphasizes the fact that the love Jane has for Rochester prevents his reliance on her from becoming a burden.

36–9 **He loved... sweetest wishes** the vocabulary in this concluding section of the extract adds to the overwhelming sense of happiness and unity. Through words such as *truly* and *fondly*, Brontë presents a pure and clear description of two people in love. The intensifying premodifier *so* emphasizes the strength of their emotions and the final image of him being willing to *indulge* her *sweetest wishes* leaves us in no doubt that Brontë wants this to be a celebration of a marriage based on mutual love and respect.

Remember: Christina Rossetti (1862)

Christina Rossetti (1830–1894) is one of the most celebrated female poets of the nineteenth century. Though her writing is full of vivid, lively imagery, her life was blighted with sadness and her poetry is often considered rather melancholy. This poem is quite typical of Rossetti's rather pessimistic yet beautifully lyrical tone.

In this sonnet she explores the grief of parting, using simple yet striking imagery. The parting may not specifically be one caused by death, however. Crucially the poem deals with a juxtaposition often seen in Rossetti's work: the conflict between her devout religious beliefs and her desire to experience love. She frequently explores her fear of going against God's will by following her desires and embarking upon a relationship, as she views this as something that could sully her pure heart and detract from her relationship with God. In this poem, the idea that she must leave her lover is presented as something that should not be mourned, though it seems tragic.

1 What sort of feelings and emotions do you feel are evoked by the opening line? Its starkness establishes a rather chilling tone to the poem and immediately foregrounds the sense of loss that will feature throughout.

2 **the silent land** the image created through this metaphor can initially be seen as quite stark, and suggestive of an empty loneliness. However, it could also be argued that the silence is a contemplative state that Rossetti craves so that she can think only of God. Using the definite article *the* may imply the grave or heaven, but also suggests that there is a certain place of quiet reflection in the mind.

3–4 What do you think about the tone established here? These lines seem to typify the uncertainty and indecision in Rossetti's confused state of mind. The echo created from the use of *turn* and *turning* underscores this confusion.

5 **Remember me** the repetition of this phrase adds to the sense that this is a lament, but also seems to suggest a certain desperation: although the lovers are to be separated, she does not wish the experience of their love to be forgotten.

9–10 The persona seems to be issuing advice to her lover here, and suggesting that he must move on from the relationship rather than *grieve* for what has been lost. The use of *grieve*, of course, is highly significant as it echoes the macabre tone the poem adopts.

11 **darkness and corruption** why do you think these abstract nouns have been used? They could suggest that dwelling on the loss of the relationship may bring bitterness and frustration.

13–14 How do these famous lines, which are often quoted in isolation, affect your response to the whole poem?

Middlemarch: George Eliot (1872)

George Eliot, whose real name was Mary Ann Evans, began writing *Middlemarch* (described by writer and critic Virginia Woolf as 'the magnificent book that, with all its imperfections, is one of the few English novels written for grown-up people') in 1869, when she was 50. Eliot was both comfortably off and at the height of her powers; her reputation as a novelist had by then eclipsed the scandal of her private life. She lived with the writer George Lewes for 24 years until his death in 1878, but the couple could not marry since Lewes was held to have condoned his wife's adultery and was therefore unable to divorce her.

Middlemarch is a multi-stranded narrative set in a Midlands town in the early 1830s, and it examines a number of themes that were topical both in the 1830s and at the time of writing. Among these themes are the position of women and the nature of marriage in the middle of the nineteenth century.

This extract is taken from near the beginning of the novel. Dorothea Brooke is a passionately religious young woman whose strict principles are severely applied to her own conduct, and to an extent that of others. Eliot is quick to point up some of Dorothea's inconsistencies, such as her pleasure in presiding over her uncle's household and enjoying the 'homage' accorded to her. But there is no doubt that Dorothea means well and is always anxious to implement useful schemes on her uncle's estate, while also craving the intellectual stimulation that is denied to her as a woman.

At the start of the book she is presented as discouraging the advances of a local young baronet. Then she meets the middle-aged clergyman Edward Casaubon, who seeks a companion to help him to finish his life's work (called *The Key to All Mythologies*) since his eyesight is failing. Seeing in him a man whose work and principles she can deeply admire, she is instantly possessed of the desire to act as his helper.

1–2 **It had now... make her his wife** this statement highlights two aspects of mid-nineteenth-century courtship. First, people of

Casaubon's and Dorothea's class and temperament had very limited opportunities to meet and form relationships leading to marriage; the characters are beginning to consider each other as potential marriage partners soon after their first encounter. Second, it makes clear that the onus is on the man to move the relationship on to the next stage; the woman occupies a passive role where she has to wait for a man to *make her* into a wife.

3–4 **a sort of reverential gratitude** Dorothea gives Casaubon almost god-like importance here.

4 **nay** this form of 'no' was becoming archaic in Eliot's time but it was still familiar from the Authorized Version of the Bible. The *winged messenger* or angel in the next line again has obvious biblical echoes.

7–8 **oppressed by… summer haze** Dorothea is presented as struggling through the vagueness that swamps her when she seeks to find something to do which will *make her life greatly effective*.

9–10 **What could she do, what ought she to do?** her desperation is emphasized by the rhetorical indirect questions.

10–11 **a budding woman** Dorothea is nineteen when the story begins and this image conveys her youth, her vitality and her potential (especially compared to the dried-up Casaubon).

12–14 **a girlish instruction… a discursive mouse** Dorothea needs both intellectual and moral stimulation and the teaching usually given to girls at the time was, as this striking image indicates, meagre, simplistic and barely coherent.

14–15 **endowment of stupidity and conceit** Eliot uses *endowment* (in its sense of a gift from God or nature) ironically here to suggest that a girl who, unlike Dorothea, was unintelligent and vain, might find *her ideal of life* and personal contentment more easily.

17 **patronage** women of Dorothea's position in society would be able to offer financial and practical support to junior clergy.

18 **'Female Scripture Characters'** a book by Frances Elizabeth King, published in 1813; characteristic of the devotional reading of young women of the period.

19 **Sara** the wife of Abraham, who bore her son Isaac when well past child-bearing age (Genesis 18:9–15, 21:1–3).

Old Dispensation the Old Testament of the Bible.
Dorcas One of the early Christians, described in Acts 9:36 as 'full of good works'. She was reputed to be an excellent needlewoman, and 'Dorcas societies' where women sewed in aid of the poor were common in Victorian times.

20–1 **care of her soul over her embroidery** sewing tended to be associated with religious piety (see above); for example, women might embroider verses from the Bible onto samplers or meet for religious discussion while sewing.

23 **being involved in affairs religiously inexplicable** stereotypically, men were less interested in religious matters than women but could partly be forgiven for this since their daily professional concerns seemed to be outside the framework of religion.

25 **poor Dorothea** Eliot becomes more intrusive as a narrator here, showing overt sympathy for her protagonist.

27–8 **ardent, theoretic and intellectually consequent** Dorothea is passionate, believes in ideas, needs to follow her thought processes to their logical conclusions.

31 **labyrinth of petty courses** Eliot uses the image of a *labyrinth* or *maze* to illustrate the bewilderment Dorothea feels when she considers what she regards as the pointless social duties of her life.

33 **exaggeration and inconsistency** by obliging herself to act according to her scrupulous conscience and to demand of herself *the completest knowledge* in everything she undertakes, Dorothea is bound to seem ridiculous or inconsistent to others.

37 **as yet** Eliot hints that, as she matures, Dorothea's *passion* will not always be directed towards hunger of the soul.

39 **girlish subjection to her own ignorance** she recognizes that she is enslaved to her own lack of knowledge and understanding.

40 **freedom of voluntary submission** Dorothea is therefore prepared to submit herself to someone whom she believes to be wiser; because this is a *voluntary* act, she feels that it still affords her *freedom*.

40–1 **a guide who would take her along the grandest path** Dorothea's ambitions are for good deeds but ones that would also have something of greatness about them.

42 **I should learn everything then** after a passage of quite dense character analysis, Eliot enlivens the narrative with Dorothea's own voice.

44 **It would be my duty to study** here Dorothea is envisaging her role as helpmeet of a man she hardly knows, enjoying the prospect of being able to perform her *duty*.

46 **our lives** she is already thinking of the two of them in the first person plural.

48 **Pascal** Blaise Pascal, a seventeenth-century French thinker, mathematician and physicist who made major contributions to scientific understanding. He abandoned science for religious philosophy after a mystical experience.

49 **great men** again, Dorothea is revealed as anxious not simply to do her duty but to be involved, at first through a man, as she seeks to marry one she views as *great*.

50 **when I got older** later, she hopes, she will be able to do great things herself, *lead a grand life here – now – in England*.

53–4 **a mission to a people whose language I don't know** this rather poignant image highlights how difficult it is for Dorothea to satisfy herself that she has discharged her duties adequately.

A Woman of No Importance: Oscar Wilde (1893)

A Woman of No Importance was written when the campaign for women's suffrage and the right to education and work were key issues for Victorian society. The woman of the title is Rachel Arbuthnot who, having been jilted by her lover Lord Illingworth 20 years before the start of the play, is confronted with the possibility that her son, Gerald (who does not know who his real father is) will become Lord Illingworth's secretary. In this passage Mrs Arbuthnot tries to explain why she is so opposed to this idea, without revealing the whole truth to Gerald.

4–6 **Gerald, come near... mother's own boy** this could be viewed as emotional blackmail, as Mrs Arbuthnot recalls her son's childhood and asserts a sense of ownership in her relationship with him.

8 **there was a girl once** Mrs Arbuthnot is, in fact, speaking about her own history.

11–12 **She knew nothing… everything** this statement illustrates the vulnerability of young women in Victorian England, presenting them as defenceless, naive and innocent, the easy prey of privileged young men.

12–13 **He made this girl love him** Mrs Arbuthnot presents herself as the victim through the word *made*, suggesting that she had no choice.

13–14 **she left her father's house with him one morning** this is an acknowledgment of a moral transgression – it was completely contrary to Victorian morality and society's attitudes to marriage.

15 **he had promised to marry her** this statement serves to illustrate her simplicity and vulnerability as a young woman.

20–1 **Before her child was born** this statement introduces the main issue of her story in an understated manner, which serves to maximize the effect of the revelation.

25–7 **her life was ruined… ruined also** the reiteration of the word *ruined* emphasizes the effect of giving birth to a child outside marriage in Victorian England. Wilde creates an image of a woman lost not just to society but to herself.

27–8 **She suffered terribly – she suffers now** the use of the past and present tenses reinforces the permanent nature of the effect on the woman's life.

31–2 **wears a mask… a leper** these terms create an image of a woman who is forced to hide the truth from everyone to avoid being shunned as if she were diseased.

32–3 **The fire… her anguish** the use of *fire* and *water* as images of purification again serve to stress the terrible sense of guilt that haunts Mrs Arbuthnot.

33–5 **Nothing… lost soul** the repeated use of exclamation marks and the staccato sentences all serve to emphasize her abject misery.

36 **That is why** the repetition of this phrase clinches the argument and seems almost to echo the rhetoric of a court of law.

38 **My dear mother** do Gerald's first words appear patronizing and hollow?

43 **No nice girl** the repetition of the empty word *nice* reveals Gerald's limited sensitivity and also reflects Victorian attitudes towards 'fallen' women.

Jude the Obscure: Thomas Hardy (1895)

Thomas Hardy was born in the hamlet of Higher Bockhampton, Dorset, in 1840 to a humble but ambitious family. Originally trained as an architect, he supplemented his basic education with private tuition and considerable wider reading and in 1867 returned home from London, where he had been working in an architectural practice, to devote himself to writing more or less full time. He always regretted that he had not attended university (as few of his background were able to do), and the story of Jude, a young stonemason who aspires to study at the university of Oxford (called Christminster in the novel) to an extent reflects Hardy's own resentment that this opportunity was routinely denied to men of his class. However, unlike Jude, whose attempts to progress academically and socially meet with miserable failure, in part due to his own weaknesses, Hardy went on to enjoy a celebrated professional life.

Hardy's relationships with women were famously complex. His union with his first wife, Emma Gifford, was strained by the time he was writing *Jude the Obscure*. Relations between the two were not improved by its publication: Emma was afraid that the public would read the book as autobiography (although Hardy hinted at various times that the female protagonist was based on his close friend, writer Florence Henniker, and his cousin Tryphena who was a teacher, with both of whom he had been professedly in love). Besides, the views which Hardy was exploring here offended Emma's strict religious principles. Given its content and ideas, shocking for the day, *Jude the Obscure* caused something of a furore on its publication and Hardy resolved to abandon novel-writing from then on, returning to his first enthusiasm and establishing himself as a very successful poet. Ironically many of his most moving poems were written on Emma's death as he dwelt on his regrets about their marriage.

The novel deals with Jude's relationship with his cousin, Sue Bridehead, with whom he falls in love although they are married to other people. Leaving their spouses, they live in lodgings separated only by a landing. Jude is anxious for their commitment to be placed on a more formal footing but Sue will consent neither to a full sexual relationship nor to marriage. Later in the novel, after Sue reneges on her promise to marry, fearing that the confines of marriage will destroy their love, they do live together as husband and wife and have two children, but tragic circumstances finally drive them apart.

1 **intimate** this refers to mental, spiritual and emotional closeness rather than physical intimacy.

6–7 **women are taught… to a man** in late Victorian times, opportunities for a woman were still limited and marriage was seen as her noblest calling. One of the many tricks a woman was encouraged to play to 'catch' a husband was to be less open than he was in expressing feelings: forthrightness in women was frowned on as unfeminine.

12 **The better class of man** despite his flaws and his miserable social status (exacerbated by public condemnation of his relations with Sue), Jude still sees himself as a man who possesses refined judgment.

12–13 **caught by airy affections of dodging and parrying** Jude's first marriage was to Arabella, a woman who tricked him into marriage by pretending to be pregnant, after seducing him into a relationship by playing hot and cold with him; hence Hardy's fencing metaphor here and Jude's scathing references to *the game of elusiveness* women such as Arabella play.

14 **Nemesis** in Greek mythology, Nemesis was the spirit of divine retribution who meted out justice, particularly to people who set themselves up against the gods and claimed more for themselves than they were due.

19–20 **a guilty look… a tragic voice** Hardy presents Sue, too, as somewhat prone to games-playing, although her wiles are less conscious than Arabella's and seem to result from her own confusion; she is torn between her wish to do right by the men in her life and her fears of commitment.

30–1 **I have nobody but you, and nobody to defend me** Sue's behaviour has been so unorthodox that she can expect no one to stand by her; and, as a woman with relatively little freedom, this isolation is alarming.

31–3 **it is *very* hard... married or no!** this is a key statement and one that caused offence to some of Hardy's readers. Though considerable numbers of people, especially of Sue's and Jude's class, lived as common-law spouses in late Victorian times, it was unacceptable to condone the practice publicly – particularly since its justification here is in the mouth of a woman.

34 **my own comrade and sweetheart** Jude presents an idealistic view of their partnership, envisaging Sue as both lover and best friend.

35 **do the other thing** Hardy is obliged to use euphemisms for sexual matters.

36 **pettish** sulky and irritable.

Dear Scott, Dearest Zelda: Zelda Fitzgerald (1919)

The book from which this extract is taken is a collection of the correspondence between Zelda and F. Scott Fitzgerald. Married in the decadent jazz age of the 1920s, the two were both eccentric writers (though her husband received far more recognition for his works both during and after their lifetimes). They lived a lavish lifestyle which frequently involved outrageous parties and plenty of alcohol. Once married, their passionate relationship was often fraught with jealousy and insecurities, and in the time before his death they saw very little of each other.

This letter was written in 1919, before they were married, and reflects their passionate nature, presenting us with a rather touching image of love. The dashes suggest that Fitzgerald is writing spontaneously and from the heart.

2 **lonesome nights** the loneliness is attributed to both of them as they await their wedding day separately.

3–4 **I am loving… day and night** this is a rather striking admission given the context of the letter, and goes against our expectations for a love letter as it suggests she is happy to be alone. However, it reminds us of the fact that the mere anticipation of seeing a loved one can create excitement and pleasure.

5–6 **when I miss you most, it's hardest to write** again this might go against our expectations about the writer of a love letter; but it is not unusual to find that while feeling most emotion it is hardest to put it into words.

8–9 **you're so sweet when you're melancholy** this reminds us that lovers often see beauty in all manner of moods.

9–10 **I love your sad tenderness** this gives a sense of his suffering, and the phrase also consolidates the notion that she loves every element of his character.

12 **Those dear, dear little fusses** the excitement of a lovers' quarrel is implicit here, yet we can see that the rather child-like vocabulary she uses plays down their disagreements, suggesting perhaps that he considers them more significant than she does.

14–15 **Scott… precious love** the direct address personalizes the sentiment and the use of the adjective *precious* highlights how important the relationship is to Fitzgerald.

16 **sordid, colorless existence** the two adjectives create a rather dark, sinister picture of a world without love.

19–20 **I want to love first, and live incidentally** the sense is that without love, life would be pointless.

22–3 **You've trusted me with the dearest heart of all** the romance of this image is doubly powerful: she acknowledges the fact that he has given his heart to her and also that it is *the dearest*; not only does she feel blessed that he has trusted her but she feels she has won the best prize.

27–8 **I'd have… decoration** here Fitzgerald objectifies herself as she believes that without love she would be empty, meaningless. What does this suggest about her views of herself?

28–9 **Don't you think I was made for you?** this image maintains the idea of her being an object or a possession, but she seems to celebrate the fact that she has been created for him.

32 **when we're alone, I want to help** it is interesting that Fitzgerald here talks about a private relationship that seems somewhat different from the public one, as when they are alone she can become his equal – helping and inspiring him rather than merely being a trinket he can admire and show *to the world*.

35 **I love you** signing the letter with such a personal and direct statement consolidates its emotional and romantic tone.

Testament of Youth: Vera Brittain (1933)

This extract is from Vera Brittain's autobiographical *Testament of Youth*. In it she recalls her life during the First World War, as a daughter, sister, lover and nurse. The passage deals with the moment she learns of the death of her fiancé Roland Leighton.

3 **exiguous** scanty, meagre.

6 **tremulous eagerness of anticipation** the balancing of *tremulous* with *eagerness* creates the sense of fear as well as excited expectation of the approaching meeting.

10 **rain pounding on the tin roof** the use of the 'pathetic fallacy' – where the weather matches the emotions of the protagonists – suggests the turbulence of the narrator's emotions while at the same time foreshadowing the tragic conclusion to all her anticipation.

14 **exultant benevolence** this phrase reinforces the all-embracing sense of goodwill her happy expectations have created.

23 **wrought up** worked up.

24 **thank whatever God might exist** note the questioning of accepted religious doctrine.

25 **supreme gift of Roland** the language here suggests a religious offering.

26–30 **The music of the organ… so poignant** note the tripling of clauses as the description builds up to reveal her mixed emotions.

31–4 **'I am the Resurrection... shall never die'** the use of religious rhetoric reinforces the all-embracing nature of her love for Roland.

40–1 **grey sea tossing rough with white surf-crested waves** the image of the sea can be read in two ways. The sea is a powerful elemental force and is often used as a metaphor for sexual passion. However, it can also be seen here as another hint of impending doom.

55–6 **pastel-blue crêpe-de-Chine blouse** the domestic detail here serves to slow the pace of the passage and maintains a sense of the personal and the ordinary.

60–3 The conclusion of the passage is deliberately understated and the language is brisk and factual, which all serve to intensify the emotional impact on the reader.

The Collector: John Fowles (1963)

The Collector was John Fowles's first novel and is quite different in subject matter from his later writing. In this book, Fowles addresses the issue of obsession, and the desire to possess and control another person.

The narrator is a lowly paid, relatively uneducated orphan, brought up by his aunt and uncle. In his youth he becomes interested in collecting butterflies; a sudden win on the football pools allows him to extend his fascination to a young art student. Miranda, the girl he pursues, is from the well-educated middle classes and under normal circumstances would be unattainable for him. This passage details the moment he captures her as she walks home alone one evening.

1–6 The passage opens with the air of a general conversation, which belies the sinister intentions of which the reader is aware. Throughout the rest of the passage we hear only the voice of the first-person narrator, and thus we are given a detailed insight into the way his mind works.

11–12 **and then I got her** the casual tone is replaced by the sudden attack, which is understated and similar to the trapping of a butterfly in a net.

15 **she struggled like the dickens** expressions such as this reveal the limited vocabulary of the narrator and the difference in education between himself and his victim.

17–19 **I looked down the road... bolt for it** the staccato rhythm demonstrates the tension of the moment and also the fear and stealth of the captor.

20–1 **I was holding her up instead of holding her quiet** here the girl is seen as the vulnerable victim; she has been silenced. By contrast the narrator seems to be empowered.

33–5 **She was still... she was all right** the passage concludes as it began with a calm, matter-of-fact tone where all the actions are described with plainness and precision.

My Mother: Jamaica Kincaid (1984)

Jamaica Kincaid was born in 1949 in Antigua and has lived in America since 1965. She has written non-fiction (especially books on travel and gardening) as well as novels, short stories, essays, a film script and numerous articles. For nine years she was a regular columnist for *The New Yorker* magazine. Currently she also teaches creative writing at Harvard University. She describes herself as 'someone who writes to save her life'.

This extract, from her collection *At the Bottom of the River*, explores one of her main themes, the relationship between mother and daughter. Kincaid's relationship with her own mother was difficult: the two were extremely close until Kincaid was nine, then the writer feels that her mother withdrew emotionally from her when her three brothers were born, though she concedes that this might have happened anyway when she entered adolescence. When she was sent to New York to work as an au pair at 16, instead of sending money home, she saved it for her education and did not even open her mother's letters. Subsequently she changed her name (she was born Elaine Potter

Richardson), partly as a way of distancing herself from her family.

Kincaid is also concerned with issues of colonialism. Antigua was a British colony until 1967 and many of the references to mothers and daughters in her work can be read as observations on the complex relationship between Britain and Antigua. In *My Mother*, Kincaid writes about how a girl deals with her mother's attempts to socialize her and explores the ways in which the daughter both resents and is proud of her mother, is angry with her and yet wants to impress her, identifies with her and yet wants to be separate from her. *My Mother* is a prose poem rather than a story and owes something to the genre of magic realism, where elements of the fantastic co-exist quite naturally with a realistic setting. Kincaid uses a number of extended metaphors to illustrate the ambivalent but intimate relationship between mother and daughter and, arguably, between a self-styled 'mother country' and its 'daughter' colony.

1 **Immediately on wishing my mother dead** this opening to the story may shock some readers, but its sentiment will be instantly recognizable to others who have experienced stormy relationships with close relatives.

2 **I was sorry** the swiftness with which the narrator feels and expresses her remorse establishes this outburst as typical of a young girl.

2–3 **cried so many... was drenched** Kincaid uses hyperbole here to emphasize the force and naivety of the girl's response.

5 **she took pity on me** the mother too seems to react in an unnecessarily dramatic way.

8 **finally I suffocated** Kincaid begins to describe the reconciliation between mother and daughter in naturalistic terms, then goes on to choose extreme imagery to convey the girl's strength of feeling and illustrate the complexity of the mother's behaviour, which seems to the girl part tender, part domineering.

lay on her bosom the repetition of *bosom* suggests that the mother still sees the girl as in need of the nurturing she required as a baby (and here, again, the subjects of the text can also be read as colonizer and colonized).

9 **for a time uncountable** the girl has made a bid for independence but, because of her youth, it has been overly aggressive; on observing her mother's reaction, she has quickly retracted it. Now the mother has the upper hand and keeps the girl by her for as long as she determines – the girl is not even aware of how long it is.

9–10 **for a reason she has kept to herself** throughout this story, the relationship between mother and daughter is presented as part mutual support system, part contest. Here the mother uses her authority to keep secrets from the girl. Again the narrative is illustrative of the relationship between colonizer and colonized, where the former decides when the latter is ready to understand and take responsibility.

10–11 **she shook me out and stood me under a tree** now the mother uses her initiative to help the daughter to gain some independence, releasing her from her reliant state. The mother does not cast her quite out into the world but places her *under a tree*, an image which suggests the nurturing power of nature.

11–12 **I cast a sharp… 'So'** the girl has matured and can see her mother as separate from herself. The adjective *sharp* indicates her new perceptiveness, perhaps mixed with harshness.

13 **Instantly I grew my own bosoms** the immediate result is a sign that she is starting to be a woman in her own right and does not need her mother to nourish her; instead, she is beginning to become a person who can nourish others. Though the girl's breasts are *small mounds at first*, they represent her growing independence and confidence. Not only can she *rest* on her own resources but she is free to decide (*if ever necessary*) when she is vulnerable.

15–16 **Between my mother and me** the girl and her mother are now more independent of each other, symbolized by the physical separation of the *small pond*, a feature that is created by the girl rather than the mother.

16 **the tears I had cried** though they can now be organized and do not drench the earth any more, the continued presence of *the tears* shows that this liberty has not been achieved without cost to the girl.

18–19 **thick and black and poisonous** the relationship between the girl and her mother is still perplexing and potentially damaging.

19 **unnamable invertebrates** this suggests issues that cannot be mentioned for fear that they will cause serious rifts.

20–1 **watched each other carefully** the two are vigilant with each other: they seem concerned to avoid hurting each other as much as in fear of being hurt.

22 **words and deeds of love and affection** realizing that they are liable to harm each other, the two must compensate by being pro-active in showing tenderness.

The Kaleidoscope: Douglas Dunn (1985)

Scottish poet and academic Douglas Dunn was born in 1942. In this poem he uses the idea of a kaleidoscope (a telescope-like instrument that uses mirrors and piece of coloured glass to create an ever-changing pattern of shapes as it is rotated) as a metaphor to reflect on his feelings about the loss of his wife; Dunn had nursed her through a long illness. He uses both past and present tense to explore the conflicting emotions of grief and the warmth and tenderness of his love for his wife. It is also interesting to note that Dunn uses a sonnet structure, as this is often chosen to present intense emotions and especially to express love.

1 **these stairs** the deictic (context-dependent) reference *these* creates a sense of the here and now, making the poem personal to Dunn's experiences.

2 **to find you pillowed with your books** this and the following two lines create a rather intimate domestic image of his wife.

5 **I might find** the auxiliary verb *might* (repeated from line 2) suggests a sense of hope: Dunn is remembering times when he would find his wife there and almost hopes he may again.

6 **your kaleidoscope** it is interesting to note that the name *kaleidoscope* comes from the Greek word *kalos* meaning beautiful, suggesting therefore the beauty of their relationship.

7 **A symmetry of husbands** this image reflects the many different ways in which his wife saw him, emphasizing the complexity of their relationship.

8 This list of three offers a sense of optimism, contrasting with those in lines 12 and 13.

10–11 **looking in/At where you died** the use of enjambment here makes the reference to his wife's deathbed stand out; the image is poignant as it works with the familiarity of the location that has been established in the poem.

12 **my flesh, my soul, my skin** there are religious undertones to this tripling, and the suggestion seems to be that Dunn has given himself wholeheartedly to his wife during her illness, becoming the food that aims to sustain her.

13–14 The concluding couplet brings us back into the present as the reference to *Grief* reminds us that his feelings of loss are still crippling. The three verbs *stand, wait* and *cry* all echo the sense of grief. He ends the poem by foregrounding the fact that the death of a loved one raises the impossible question *why*.

One Flesh: Elizabeth Jennings (1987)

Born in 1926, Elizabeth Jennings read English at Oxford and lived there for most of her life, working as a city librarian, publisher's reader and reviewer, as well as being a prolific poet, the author of over 20 volumes. A friendly but intensely private person, who disliked literary gatherings and poetry readings, she wrote poems on love, loss, art, death and faith, dealing with these themes with tenderness, subtlety and sensitivity, and not omitting to explore painful areas of her own experience, such as her bouts of mental illness. She died in 2001.

Jennings was linked by some critics to an important group of poets who came to prominence around the 1950s and were dubbed 'The Movement'. These poets, who included Philip Larkin, D.J. Enright, Kingsley Amis and Thom Gunn, set out to write poetry which was simpler, more rational, lucid and carefully crafted than the poems of the previous decade. Jennings was ambivalent about being associated with this group and, indeed, her work is less cynical and self-consciously witty than theirs.

This poem, about the poet's parents, is one of Jennings's most famous works. The title recalls words from Genesis 2:24, where it is said that a married couple 'shall be one flesh'. Here Jennings writes understatedly about what has happened to the relationship between her parents over the years of their partnership.

1 With an irregular metre compared to the generally conventional pentameters of the rest of the poem, Jennings tells us baldly that the two no longer share a bed.

2 **keeping the light on late** the man seems more concerned with his *book* than his wife, even to the extent of disturbing her sleep.

3–4 **like a girl dreaming of childhood/All men elsewhere** by using this simile, Jennings takes the woman back to her pre-marital innocence where sexual experience was some time in the future.

5–6 **Some new event** though Jennings expresses this idea as a simile (using *as if*), she insinuates that the *new event* for which the couple *wait* – the prospect of which interrupts the man's reading – is an actual one.

6 The *shadows overhead* are literal, but her *fixed* stare suggests that they also represent the death of one or both partners.

7 **flotsam** refuse or debris floating on the surface of the sea.
a former passion Jennings implies that the passionate feelings they once shared are so firmly in the past that they may as well have been experienced in a previous relationship, not with each other.

9–10 **like a confession… or too much** so infrequent are gestures of affection between the couple that, when they do occur, they are obvious signals of how lacking physical love is in their relationship. Perhaps this reminder is even dangerous.

11–12 **a destination… a preparation** this statement may also indicate that the afterlife for which the two have been preparing will (as conventional Christian teaching suggests) be chaste.

13 In this key line, Jennings achieves an oxymoronic effect by linking *apart* and *close together* by the repetition of *strangely*, to convey the idea that the couple's apartness is odd because they should be more noticeably close to each other, and their closeness is odd because their ease with each other communicates as much intimacy as more overt shows of affection might; putting these together, it is odd that their demeanour indicates both separateness and closeness at the same time.

14–15 **like a thread to hold/And not wind in** this simile demonstrates how the *silence* between the couple acts as *a thread* which both keeps them together and prevents them from becoming closer.

15 **time itself's a feather** this metaphor leads into the final rhetorical question which starts *Do they know they're old*. The implication here is that the two have aged so gradually and imperceptibly that they have not noticed how old they have grown.

17 In her compassionate yet detached exploration of her parents' relationship, this is Jennings's first identification of her link to them.

18 In an elegant metaphor, Jennings describes the austere reality of her parents' lives, making their situation personal to herself, since she is a product of the passion that was once between them. How do you respond to this line?

Clearances 5: Seamus Heaney (1987)

Seamus Heaney is an Irish poet born in 1939, who was awarded the Nobel prize for literature in 1995. Heaney often uses the ordinary and everyday to explore complex emotions and ideas. In this poem, which forms part of a series called *Clearances*, Heaney explores the relationship between mother and son through the image of taking the sheets in from the washing line.

1 **The cool that came off sheets** this description engages the

reader with the sensory experience of the poet while describing a simple domestic task.

6 **like a sail in a cross-wind** this simile creates a sense of movement and journeying, related to the distance the poet at times feels between himself and his mother.

7 **dried-out undulating thwack** this onomatopoeic description recreates the crisp, clean sound as the sheets are shaken out.

8 This line evokes the mother/child relationship: one of interdependence, and working together to create a whole.

11–12 **just touch and go… holding back** this develops the idea touched on in the earlier lines, as it engages with the subtlety of the emotions between mother and son and the need to remain close while at the same time moving further away from each other.

13 **I was x and she was o** this striking image suggests the complex pattern of relationships, as it uses the terms of the game of noughts and crosses; sometimes players can make the pattern fit, but at other times it remains fragmented.

14 These details reveal the hard work and thrift of the mother in overcoming poverty. What effect do you feel they have in the context of the whole poem?

First Love: Carol Ann Duffy (1993)

Born in 1955 in Glasgow, but mainly brought up in Stafford, Carol Ann Duffy began her creative career as a playwright but is most famous for her collections of poetry. One of the best-known contemporary poets, she often challenges readers' ideas and presents common themes such as love and marriage from a very different viewpoint. Here, in a poem from her collection *Mean Time*, she offers an insight into first love by using a reflective narrative and focusing on images of the past as they recall old sentiments.

1 **a dream of first love forming real words** the contrast between *dream* and *real* here is striking, as it suggests that the *dream* of the past is colliding with the here and now.

2 **close to my lips** the reference to the lips provides an obvious sensual undertone but Duffy is most significantly using the image to emphasize the closeness of the lovers.

I speak your name this direct statement is loaded as it seems that, for the narrator, the act of saying her lover's name brings the memory to life.

4 **naked** the memory strips her of any defence she may have had: she is naked, and this gives her the chance to look more closely at the memory as she is gazing out of *the window*.

5 **a garden shaking with light** this phrase could be seen as both literal and metaphorical. The lit garden may indeed be full of movement but the image may also mean that the persona is seeing things differently and that this light is filling the vision with excitement and anticipation.

6 **This was a child's love** beginning the stanza with a reference to the past highlights the sense that the poem is about a memory. It also suggests the innocence of the love being explored.

clench a rather child-like verb, this also suggests innocence and naivety.

8 **an old film played at a slow speed** a reminder of the fact that this is a memory coming to life, this image conjures a sense of nostalgia like that conveyed by the flickering films of the past.

9–10 This list of ways in which the narrator's memory of her first love will haunt her presents us with some interesting images. The *changing sky* gives us a sense of movement and the *mirrors* suggest that the persona will see her lover reflected in herself. The phrase *wherever you are* may refer to her current love (the one mentioned in *my lover's eyes*), and could suggest that it is this lover's absence that has prompted the thoughts of her first love, but it could also be indicating the remembered lover, whom the persona will see everywhere.

11 **a star, long dead** Duffy uses the image of the star as a metaphor for the relationship, which is also *long dead* but still making an impression on the persona.

12 **tear** this suggests the impact is a sad one.

out of a dream the reference to a *dream* gives the poem a cyclical feel, as if the persona is haunted continuously by the memory.

13 **stammers** this implies both that the *love-letter* is being read aloud and that the reader is nervous, making the image of the lover even more real.

14–15 **Unseen... sweeten the air** this image can be seen in two ways. First, the flowers link to the image of the garden in the first stanza and so add to the cyclical nature of the poem as well as echoing the way in which the memory has blossomed. Second, the image could be a metaphor for the relationship with the first love, describing the sexual awakening it brought.

Daffodils: Ted Hughes (1998)

Born in Mytholmroyd, a small town in West Yorkshire in 1930, Ted Hughes was one of the foremost poets of the twentieth century and served as Poet Laureate from 1984 until his death in 1998. He wrote children's books as well as challenging, evocative, often difficult poetry. His personal life, particularly his marriage to the American poet Sylvia Plath, has been widely documented. Plath committed suicide in 1963 at the age of 30, leaving Hughes with two young children. Hughes refused to discuss their life together publicly until he published his collection *Birthday Letters*, from which this poem is taken. The collection explores aspects of Plath's personality and their life together and is dedicated to their children; their daughter, Frieda, provided illustrations for its cover.

1 In this opening question Hughes addresses an anonymous person, who is in fact his late wife, Sylvia Plath.

2 This strikes a very personal note and creates a sense of intimacy.

4–5 **She has forgotten... remember you** these lines seem almost cruel in their suggestion that Plath's life as a mother has been negated.

8 **Boss-eyed** cross-eyed.

9–10 These lines in parentheses link the death of *the grocer* to the death of his wife in a matter-of-fact tone. It could be read as the voice of a man coming to terms with the terrible divide that death creates.

17–18 **Still nomads… our whole possession** Hughes uses the idea of the desire to create *profit* through the sale of the daffodils to explore the complexity of the intimate relationship the couple shared. On the one hand he presents the relationship as still in nascent form, unsettled and distant, but on the other there is a sense of coming to terms with all that they possessed in one another.

18–19 **The daffodils… gilding of the deeds** Hughes suggests that the daffodils were an unexpected bonus to their lives. In all the plans they had created they had not taken account of the daffodils until they arrived almost like a gift from heaven (*Treasure trove*).

23–24 **Our lives… live forever** the possibilities, optimism and arrogance of youth are suggested in this line.

25 **fleeting glance of the everlasting** once again Hughes uses the image of the daffodils to explore the transient nature of the couple's life together as he ruefully considers their failure to notice that the daffodils had only a short life span.

29–30 The carelessness with which the couple treated the daffodils is considered in retrospect to be a reflection of the lack of understanding they had of each other and how limited their time would be together. Rather than being a gift from nowhere the daffodils are presented as being a *blessing* before death.

31 **So we sold them** as a result of not seeing what the daffodils represented, the couple sold them for profit, rather than enjoying them for their beauty. Again there are allusions to the failure to treasure their time together.

33–9 **You bent at it… Opened too early** the sensual language here suggests a sexual encounter but one that concludes with a feeling of being too young, too unworldly for the demands the world places on relationships.

43–4 In this vivid description of the cut stems of the daffodils, Hughes uses alliteration on the plosive 'p' and 'b' sounds to create a harsh image of the ravaged flowers.

48–9 Here Hughes seems to be suggesting that the earth is like a cold grave from which these beautiful, flame-like flowers emerge and act as a means of purification.

50 This is a blunt and uncompromising statement about the brutality of the action and the motives behind the harvesting of the crop.

56–8 **Baby-cries… wings of the year** these metaphors conjure up the vulnerability of the flowers as they force their way up out of the cold earth, dancing in the cold of the early spring weather.

60 The poem returns to its opening message, that although the individual is forgotten, nature's cycle continues unperturbed.

63–7 In the concluding stanza the scissors come to represent the distance between life and death, and the mystery of death. *Wherever they are… somewhere*, they sink deeper into the earth, while the daffodils push up into the light. The permanence of death is presented almost as a source of security, an *anchor*, and the *cross of rust* formed by the blades promises ultimate salvation. Do you feel the suggestion of consolation is as strong as the sense of desolation?

Pygmalion's Bride: Carol Ann Duffy (1999)

Carol Ann Duffy's work often expresses feminist ideas. In *The World's Wife*, the collection in which this poem appears, Duffy has re-imagined a number of famous tales and situations from history, popular culture, the Bible, literature, folklore and mythology from the points of view of their female participants rather than that of the generally more prominent male hero. In giving these overlooked women a voice, she has said that her aim has been to restore 'an obvious missing female perspective'.

In this poem, as in several others in *The World's Wife*, Duffy portrays a relationship in which a man seeks to fashion his female partner according to his own needs, and describes the woman's response to the man's controlling actions. The story of Pygmalion, which serves as the basis for this poem, is drawn from Greek myth and has inspired sculptures, paintings and, perhaps most famously, George Bernard Shaw's reinterpretation in his play *Pygmalion*, which in turn was reworked as the musical (and later film) called *My Fair Lady*.

The myth deals with a sculptor from Cyprus who, finding the women available to him too promiscuous for his liking, turns his back on love; instead he chooses a piece of ivory and carves for himself an ideal woman. She is so beautiful that he falls in love with her, clothes her and bedecks her with jewels. He prays to the goddess Aphrodite to bring her to life and Aphrodite, seeing the sculpture as a depiction of herself, forgives his crimes against love and grants his wish. In the original the couple lead a blissful married life and have two children.

The poem takes the form of a dramatic monologue. Duffy constructs a credible voice for her protagonist by using very short, disjointed lines and, often, short sentences, interspersed with occasional much longer lines. Repetition and irregular, sometimes internal, rhyme and pararhyme give emphasis to the protagonist's thoughts and feelings.

1 Throughout the poem Duffy maintains an ambiguity about the identity of the speaker – is she a real woman, or a statue? The implied comparison is used to pose questions about the objectification of women. The narrator's choice of coldness to introduce herself suggests that she is to be seen in terms of her sexual behaviour towards a man, and the mention of the material from which Pygmalion's statue was made highlights the sense that she owes her being to a man.

2 As a statue she will obviously be unresponsive, but details of the statue's thinking processes throughout the poem, as here, indicate that her impassiveness is an act.

3 Her wishes are disregarded, implying that she is powerless to stop him. The simple understatement of this line makes the narrator's plight seem more alarming.

4–8 Duffy's description of the behaviour of the man (unnamed, apart from in the title) shows him to be predatory. Despite her *stone-cool* demeanour towards him, he insists on touching her, the term *thumbed* particularly connoting disrespect. Like many victims of abuse, she plays dead in an attempt at self-preservation.

9–11 Clearly a person who is more at home with actions than words, the man eventually talks to her but his words are *blunt endearments*. Duffy extends the line here to convey a sense of the man's inarticulateness, making *what he'd do and how* seem all the more *terrible*.

12–14 Once again the narrator tries to ignore him: imagining her ears as *shells* (recalling the birth of Aphrodite, sprung from a shell at her father Zeus's command) she claims to have *heard the sea* as many people fancifully do when they put a shell to their ears.

17–18 Continuing to characterize the male as oafish, Duffy then shows him buying presents, mere trinkets without any obvious value.

22 ***girly things*** he is scornful and patronizing.

25 **shtum** the colloquialism implies a collusion – perhaps with the reader – over a situation that is being concealed.

26–33 The man's determination becomes more sinister. As he turns more vicious, he also looks for signs to prove to himself that he is having an effect on her.

30 **purple hearts** the name of a prestigious US military medal, and the street term for a recreational drug, is used here as a euphemism for bruises.

31 **inky stars** again, the impression is given that these marks would be pretty rather than ominous.

smudgy this adjective underlines the furtive status of the *clues*.

34 Again he treats her as an object, this time a doll.

35–7 What seems finally to wear the protagonist down is not the man's actions but his words, which are as abrasive as *gravel*.

38 His victory is shown by Duffy's use of paradox and simple colour metaphor.

39–49 Duffy implies that the man was intimidated by the statue-woman seizing the initiative, which he has always felt was his to take – he cannot cope as she begins dictating new terms for their relationship.

Four Letter Word – New Love Letters: eds Joshua Knelman and Rosalind Porter (2007)

This extract is from a text compiled by Joshua Knelman and Rosalind Porter, who asked a range of contemporary writers to produce a modern equivalent of the love letter. They became interested in the idea of reviving the form as, with the rise of email and text messaging, they believed it to be a dying art. This letter, written by the American poet Matthew Zapruder (born in 1967), describes the first meeting of a couple from the man's perspective, in what is a rather personal insight into the emotions associated with a first meeting.

4 **You** the narrative structure established here makes the female character the centre of attention and creates a personal tone.

6–10 **below your short... a smile** the detail in the description here is striking as the persona recalls *one tiny freckle* and the way her face was illuminated. The memory is vivid.

11 **I could see it so clearly** the *it* in this sentence could refer to the *freckle* or the *smile* that ended the previous paragraph. However, as the writer goes on to describe how this meeting changed him, the reference is more likely to mean that on reflection, he can see how his new feelings have changed things for him.

11–14 **All last year...paddle-boats** the extended metaphor here is used to describe the way in which the narrator, before this meeting, had little excitement in his life; his love has broken his passivity and woken his senses.

16–17 **the problem... love with love** this reflective comment contrasts appropriately with the rest of the piece, as it suggests that people have a rather hollow and selfish view of love.

22–3 **trying hard not to watch you laughing** what do you find striking about this recognizable image? How does it successfully convey the narrator's feelings towards the woman?

30–1 **Many things... end of the night** the non-specific *Many things* is noticeable, as the only detail we are really given about the evening centres on the 'you' of the letter.

31–2 **You may… by the door** this humorous description is memorable for its simplicity and modesty, but also helps to further establish the charm of the writer.

35–6 **clumsily looking… terrifying altitude** what is striking about the vocabulary here? How do the words seem to echo the emotions of first love and capture the conflicting feelings of excitement and fear?

38 **write it on my hand** the simple action is a beautiful symbol of love and is used as a representation of the impulsive behaviours associated with the giddiness of love.

Interpretations

Themes and ideas

The literature of love has taken many different forms and addressed countless different facets of the topic down the ages. In this section we will discuss all the extracts chosen for this book under headings that explore the many and varied aspects of love in literature.

We start with the theme of **Romance and Passion**, which deals with both spiritual and physical facets of love. Under the topic **Love and Marriage**, we examine how love is celebrated and sometimes institutionalized through religious and civil rites. By contrast, down the ages people have experienced love that is forbidden or outside social norms, and we investigate these issues under **Illicit Love**. The theme of **Unrequited Love** is a familiar one in all literature, and many writers have aimed to describe the sufferings experienced by those whose love is rejected. In any love relationship, **Meetings and Partings** are of great significance, and we examine how writers have communicated the impact of these special moments.

Other types of love include that experienced within the family, especially the parent–child relationship, and we discuss these in the section **Parents and Family**. Finally, in **God, Nature and Country**, we examine how writers are often inspired by love for an idea or concept greater than themselves.

Romance and passion

Romantic love is perhaps the most obvious area to consider when looking at writing about love through the ages. Romance is sometimes sought for its own sake, but sexual passion is usually linked to it and men and women seek to express their desires in many different ways. We will look at how the following extracts explore some of these issues:

- *The Miller's Tale*: Geoffrey Chaucer
- *Antony & Cleopatra*: William Shakespeare
- *Edward II*: Christopher Marlowe
- *The Eve of St Agnes*: John Keats
- *Testament of Youth*: Vera Brittain
- *First Love*: Carol Ann Duffy
- *Pygmalion's Bride*: Carol Ann Duffy
- *The Clod and the Pebble*: William Blake
- *Sonnet 18*: William Shakespeare
- *Dear Scott, Dearest Zelda*: Zelda Fitzgerald

In *The Miller's Tale* we are introduced to the passions of Nicholas and Alisoun as they express their desire for a sexual liaison. Throughout the passage Nicholas is presented as cunning and having more than one motive. He uses a direct and uncompromising approach as a way to attain his desires, and Chaucer uses explicit language to describe Nicholas's actions.

Activity

How does Chaucer convey Nicholas's passion in the extract from *The Miller's Tale*? How is Alisoun's response to his advances presented?

Discussion

From the outset it is made clear what Nicholas's intentions are as Chaucer describes how he begins to *rage and pleye* with Alisoun when her husband is away. Nicholas wastes no time in grabbing at Alisoun's body, yet throughout the passage Chaucer humorously parodies the formalities of courtly love as Nicholas claims he will suffer imminent death if his desires are not satisfied. To express his joy when Alisoun promises to become his lover, he doesn't use words of love but instead, we are told, he *thakked hire aboute the lendes weel*. The final description of the way Nicholas plays his musical instrument simulates the way he intends to conduct the sexual encounter, and gives a humorous picture of the energy of his passion.

Alisoun has been described as a *yonge wyf* and her immediate response to Nicholas is to express shock and to insist that she will call out for help. However, her protestations seem rather weak and lacking in conviction. Her only objection seems to be that she would be found out by her husband: *Myn housbonde is so ful of jalousie*. Thus she is presented as complicit in Nicholas's plan as she clearly wishes to experience the delights of a sexual liaison, and once this objection is overcome she is ready to accept his advances.

A woodcut based on a portrait miniature of Chaucer from the Ellesmere manuscript of *The Canterbury Tales*

In *Antony & Cleopatra*, Antony's passion is clear from the beginning of the extract, where we learn from Philo about Antony's obsession with Cleopatra, which is causing him to neglect his military duties. In Philo's opinion Antony is so preoccupied that he has lost the respect of his men and his capacity to fight. Philo presents the love in demeaning terms, referring to Antony as *a strumpet's fool*.

We may regard their love in rather a different light when we see the two characters appear together on stage. Cleopatra questions Antony's rather hyperbolic declarations of love and her astute political mind remains focused on her role, whereas Antony refuses to listen to the messenger, choosing to follow his heart instead. Shakespeare shows that we can either be led by the heart or the head, and presents the difficulty of being a successful lover and skilful ruler at the same time.

Activity

Comment on the language and imagery used by Shakespeare to present Antony's passion in the extract from *Antony & Cleopatra*.

Discussion

The language Antony uses is both direct and hyperbolic; he refers to the extremes of *beggary*, *heaven*, and *earth*. When the Messenger enters, Cleopatra uses images associated with politics and political rule, which emphasize Antony's disregard for his responsibilities. There is also a sense of his rejection of wealth and the trappings of power as he declares that his love forms *The nobleness of life*, and that in contrast to the palaces of a ruler, love creates his true home: *Here is my space*. His desire to enjoy the pleasures of life with Cleopatra suggests the intensity of their love; Antony appears to be consumed by her and can think of doing nothing but to be with her.

The passage from *Edward II* also explores passionate love, as the audience is presented with Gaveston's passion for Edward. The language used suggests *wanton* encounters and it is made clear that Gaveston is able to *draw the pliant King which way I please.* Here, then, passion seems to involve exercising control over the loved one, as Gaveston details the deep knowledge he has of the king.

Activity

What particular words or phrases suggest sexual passion in the extract from *Edward II*?

Discussion

Here is a suggested list:

- *wanton poets*
- *sylvan nymphs*
- *satyrs grazing*
- *goat-feet dance an antic hay*
- *hair that gilds the water as it glides*
- *Crownets of pearl about his naked arms*
- *sportful hands*
- *hide those parts that men delight to see*
- *peeping through the grove*
- *pulled down, and seem to die*

The line *goat-feet dance an antic hay* suggests an anarchic scene as goats are traditionally symbols of lust, and the image of pagan dancing (often associated with fertility rites) removes the experience from the life of the court to a world of unrestrained natural passions.

The image of pearls wreathed about the *naked arms* of a young boy creates a decadent picture, with the word *naked* adding sexual tension to the description.

Peeping suggests secrecy, and seeing things that are usually hidden. The image of *the grove* implies a pastoral scene, again distancing the encounter from the constraints of courtly life and social convention.

Activity

Compare the ways the extracts from *Edward II* and *The Miller's Tale* deal with passion as a selfish emotion.

Discussion

In both extracts we are presented with characters who seek self-gratification, with little fear of the consequences. Gaveston appears arrogant and self-seeking. The fact that Edward is his king does not deter a man who insists that the power in the relationship resides with him. Similarly Alisoun and Nicholas pursue their passion at the cost of marriage vows and with no feelings of loyalty towards the man who is Alisoun's husband and Nicholas's landlord.

Chaucer gives Nicholas dual intentions: he wants both to enjoy Alisoun and to make a fool of the carpenter. In *Edward II*, however, the emotions expressed in Gaveston's soliloquy as he anticipates being reunited with his lover are more complex than those seen in *The Miller's Tale*. His motives, like those of Nicholas, seem almost entirely selfish, but nevertheless there is a real sense of a desire to please Edward. Marlowe presents Gaveston as a character who wishes to exploit his power over the king (*draw the pliant King which way I please*), but he has a deep knowledge of the king and how to gratify his whims.

There are overt sexual references in both extracts, although Marlowe's description is couched in classical analogies and metaphors, whereas Chaucer is blunt and uncompromising in his choice of language, particularly when describing Nicholas's actions: *prively he caughte hire by the queynte*.

In *Edward II* the extract is a soliloquy, and therefore we learn about the imagination and desires of only one of the protagonists. In contrast we are given a detailed account by Chaucer of the behaviour and reactions of both Nicholas and Alisoun in their very physical encounter.

There is also a difference in the way the consequences of the passionate liaisons are considered in the extracts. Gaveston makes no allusion to Isabella, Edward's wife, or the impact his adultery might have on her, neither does he consider how his behaviour might endanger Edward's hold on power. In contrast, Chaucer shows Nicholas to be very clear about the effect his behaviour will have on John the carpenter, and similarly Alisoun is also very conscious of her own rather more vulnerable position should she be found out.

John Keats explores a passionate romance of a more traditional kind in his poem *The Eve of St Agnes*. Porphyro is presented as a man who is torn between adoration of the virginal Madeline and a burning sexual passion. On the one hand Porphyro is seen as pious as he kneels at Madeline's bedside as if it were an altar, *with joinèd hands and piteous eye*. On the other hand, he is an intruder into the *woofèd fantasies* of Madeline's dream world, one that he ultimately brings to an end as, *Beyond a mortal man impassioned far*, he melts *Into her dream* and achieves *Solution sweet*.

Activity

In what ways does Keats present romance in the extract from *The Eve of St Agnes*?

Discussion

Throughout the extract Keats uses a romantic tone and Gothic setting to present the coming together of these two young lovers. Madeline is desperate to see an image of her lover in her dreams and her wish is fulfilled as she wakes to find him close by. Her fear for Porphyro's well-being, and the unexpected poignancy of her grief at seeing him, contribute to the romance of the moment, with lines such as *Give me that voice again, my Porphyro*. The rich and sensual language, from the description of the fruits in the first stanza to the moment in the last stanza when Porphyro melts *Into her dream... as the rose/Blendeth its odour with the violet*, serves to conjure up a world of love that is for the moment protected from the trials of the real world.

In Vera Brittain's *Testament of Youth*, however, the world intrudes tragically on romance and passion. Unlike *The Eve of St Agnes*, which is related chiefly from a male perspective, *Testament of Youth* offers the point of view of a young woman who is very much in love. Words such as *exultant*, *mounting joy* and *harmony* all suggest a woman filled with anticipation and experiencing a sense of peace within herself and in her relationship with those around her. Roland is described as a *supreme gift*, which again reveals the strength of her emotion.

The writer Vera Brittain in her nurse's uniform

Activity

Consider the way romance is explored in *Testament of Youth*, compared with the way it is presented in *The Eve of St Agnes.*

Discussion

In *The Eve of St Agnes*, Porphyro's idea of romance seems to be self-orientated. He is, after all, an uninvited guest in Madeline's bedchamber. Madeline's response is to be afraid and question the reality of what she is seeing. Vera Brittain, however, celebrates every aspect of the real Roland and the reader is caught up in her joyful anticipation of his imminent arrival: *Already I could count, perhaps even on my fingers, the hours that must pass before I should see him.*

Porphyro's passion overpowers Madeline's fears but her insistence that *if thou diest, my Love, I know not where to go* echoes the unspoken sentiment of Brittain who, although her grief is not detailed, leaves the reader in no doubt that she will be bereft without Roland.

Carol Ann Duffy's poem *First Love* presents a love affair only indirectly but does create a sense of burning desire; the idea that love lives on is clear. Duffy, like many poets, uses metaphor and imagery to illustrate past emotions and desires. Images such as the *star* and the *flowers* link to traditional romantic symbols, yet Duffy presents them in a contemporary way. The relationship that the poem recalls was clearly a passionate one, powerful enough to reverberate in the present.

In Duffy's poem *Pygmalion's Bride*, with its fascinating twist on the Pygmalion myth, there is little romance and the passion is all on the male side. Duffy explores the situation of a woman who is the subject of unrelenting sexual harassment at the hands of a man for whom she feels nothing. He paws her, so anxious to make some impression on her that his *nails* become *claws* against her skin; but eventually it is the sheer tediousness of his words (he *jawed all night... He talked white black*) that drives the protagonist to play him at his own game. Intriguingly it is this behaviour, when she pretends to experience uncontrollable passion and acts *hot* and *wild*, that frightens the man off.

William Blake's *The Clod and the Pebble* has sometimes been portrayed as showing a stereotypically feminine form of love, through the words of the self-sacrificing Clod, and a stereotypically aggressive masculine view, through the Pebble. However, this is a rather simplistic reading, and Blake is careful to make both speakers gender-neutral. What he does imply, by paralleling the first and third stanza, is how easy it is for a love that begins as, or purports to be, selfless to become a controlling force.

Blake also may be implying criticism of a lover who adopts a submissive, self-sacrificing role in a relationship, which may be seen as the opposite of passion. In *One Flesh*, Elizabeth Jennings writes about the absence of passion in her parents' relationship now, as they are *Lying apart*, failing to engage physically with each other. This leads her to reflect on her own origins in their past passion, the *fire from which I came*.

The sonnet structure is often used to present romance and passion, as its short form and well-defined structure offer a framework for the expression of intense feelings. In his *Sonnet 18*, Shakespeare takes the traditional technique – that of comparing a loved one with something of beauty – and offers a rather different perspective, as he challenges straightforward views about the inevitable fading of physical desirability. The passion felt for the recipient of the poem seems to resonate through the types of natural beauty that Shakespeare lists, so this sonnet focuses on both the physical and the eternal aspects of love.

Activity

Comment on what you think Shakespeare's *Sonnet 18* says about the importance of physical attraction for romance and passion.

Discussion

By using images suitable for love poetry, such as comparisons to the *darling buds of May*, and drawing attention to their shortcomings as romantic metaphors, Shakespeare is in many ways parodying the type of verse that focuses solely on praising the loved one's physical appearance. Claims such as *thy eternal summer shall not fade* emphasize a belief that love and beauty can be immortalized in verse, and that physical attraction may be short lived but true passion will be able to preserve something of its essence.

It is important to consider how the form of each extract impacts on the presentation of love. The letter format, for example, is a natural one for expressing personal feelings, and is perhaps the most intimate way in which heartfelt emotions can be communicated. There is certainly evidence of this in Zelda Fitzgerald's letter to her future husband, from *Dear Scott, Dearest Zelda*. The personal nature of this particular letter gives us the sense of a spontaneous outpouring of passion. The feelings here, however, are not as we would perhaps expect, as they are driven by the couple's separation rather than focusing on the next time they will be together. Fitzgerald uses images of darkness to describe life without her partner – she speaks of *lonesome nights*, and says that being without him permanently would be *like going blind* – rather than using images of beauty to reflect on their life together. This technique reflects the rather unconventional relationship the two shared, which is reinforced by the comments that show her delight in the feeling that she has been *ordered* for and *delivered* to Scott, and wanting him to *wear me, like a watch-charm*.

Love and marriage

Many writers throughout the ages have looked at the institution of marriage and its relationship to love. As society's perception of relations between the sexes changes, so too does the fundamental issue of the marriage contract. We therefore see more traditional presentations, based on gender roles and often emphasizing the nature of duty, evolve into more contemporary views that communicate the ideal of equality in marriage. Though more modern texts reflect the varied and diverse family structures of contemporary society, it can be seen that the presentation of a loving marriage still interests writers and readers alike. In this section we will focus on the following extracts from the collection:

- *Much Ado About Nothing*: William Shakespeare
- *Jane Eyre*: Charlotte Brontë
- *Middlemarch*: George Eliot
- *The Kaleidoscope*: Douglas Dunn

Courtship and marriage are important themes in *Much Ado About Nothing*. In the extract, although the marriage under discussion is one that society will endorse, Shakespeare is keen to emphasize Claudio's passion. He presents a young soldier who is under the spell of an initial physical attraction, and seems to celebrate the impulsive behaviour that often brings people together. This extract shows only the male perspective as the friends speak of the steps they will take towards the eventual marriage without any consideration for the woman's feelings: *the conclusion is, she shall be thine*. The rest of the play shows that reaching this conclusion is not so straightforward as they think.

Charlotte Brontë presents a much more radical view of marriage in *Jane Eyre*. At the time of publication, a marriage between Jane and Rochester would have been considered the only acceptable 'happy ending' for the text. Some commentators believe that Brontë's original ending to the novel did not reunite the two but left Jane as an independent, financially secure female, and that Brontë was persuaded to change the ending by her publisher to introduce a traditional conclusion. Whether or not this is true, like many other female writers through time, Brontë is keen to maintain her protagonist's independence while not wanting to detract from the loving relationship of hero and heroine. Jane is therefore liberated within the marriage. The female voice is clear, confident and determined, qualities that are established throughout the novel and which help the reader believe that Jane would indeed be an equal in the marriage.

An interesting comparison can be made between this text and the extract from *Middlemarch*, which is set (although not written) around the time Brontë composed *Jane Eyre*. In George Eliot's novel the protagonist begins by accepting a subordinate position within marriage – she hopes it will bring her the education and the purpose she craves. In this extract Dorothea is more than happy to see herself as the mere helper of the person she envisages as *almost… a winged messenger*, even thinking *How good of him* when he appears to be considering her as a wife. Since her experience of intellectual and spiritual education has been so limited, she is eager to depend on a learned man such as Casaubon to *deliver her from her girlish subjection to her own ignorance*. To an extent she means to live through him, to advance herself only so that she *might help him the better in his great works*. But interestingly Dorothea, of whom her uncle a little later in the novel says *I thought you liked your own opinion*, is also determined to use her husband's knowledge to construct an integrity of her own: *And then I should know what to do, when I got older*.

The turbulent relationship of Jane Eyre and Edward Rochester (seen here in a 2006 stage adaptation) leads to a harmonious marriage

Activity

Compare the presentation of Jane Eyre's and Dorothea Brooke's views of married love in the extracts.

Discussion

Jane Eyre is an orphan who has few prospects, and in the majority of the novel she is learning to live independently, whereas it is made clear from the outset that Dorothea is an attractive heiress who can expect to marry. This is one reason why the two reveal very different approaches to marriage. While both idealize marriage and the unity between husband and wife (Jane describes their *perfect concord*), they have a very dissimilar notion of the sort of closeness marriage will bring. The traditionally inferior position of the female is intensified by the fact that both women are much younger than their spouses; but Jane sees herself as her husband's equal (though it is noteworthy that this equality is only achieved when he becomes disabled), while Dorothea seizes the role of pupil enthusiastically, though it is clear that she wishes to learn from her husband as much for her own purposes as for his, saying *And then I should know what to do, when I got older*.

The Kaleidoscope, the most modern of the texts studied in this section, also presents a rather traditional view of marriage, but it is framed by the sadness of bereavement. Douglas Dunn's poem is a beautiful presentation of love within marriage, and its personal tone and setting give it an intimate feel. Despite being about loss, the poem is a celebration of the couple's marriage and its beauty.

Activity

Note the literary devices and techniques used by Dunn in *The Kaleidoscope* to create a sense of his loving marriage.

Discussion

Here are some ideas about the poem's presentation of the couple's loving relationship.

- The use of *The Kaleidoscope* as the title of the poem refers to the many different elements of the relationship between Dunn and his wife, and evokes a vibrant image of the couple's love.
- Dunn uses descriptions of a simple domestic environment (*these stairs, a tray, your books*) in order to emphasize the everyday beauty of the relationship.
- The two examples of tripling towards the end of the poem (*my flesh, my soul, my skin* and *I stand, and wait, and cry*) illustrate the husband's unchanging dedication to his wife.
- The use of direct address (*you*) also emphasizes just how personal the poem is and reminds us of the fact that the images and emotions presented are unique to this couple.
- The blending of past and present tenses throughout the poem suggests that powerful memories make the relationship a permanent reality, in defiance of death.

Illicit love

Love that is outside the limits of the socially acceptable can be the most testing in terms of commitment and integrity. All love requires individuals to share aspects of themselves, but illicit love often requires greater sacrifices and in consequence makes those involved more vulnerable. Writers have for centuries found this situation fascinating, not only because they frequently like to challenge readers' notions of what is appropriate and what is not, but also because their characters' very vulnerability can force them into self-knowledge and eloquence.

In this section we will look at:

- *The Miller's Tale*: Geoffrey Chaucer
- *Edward II*: Christopher Marlowe
- *A Woman of No Importance*: Oscar Wilde
- *Jude the Obscure*: Thomas Hardy
- *The Collector*: John Fowles
- *'Tis Pity She's a Whore*: John Ford

Throughout *The Miller's Tale*, Chaucer presents the illicit love between Nicholas and Alisoun in a humorous, light-hearted way. Both characters seem to have only self-interest at heart and although Alisoun's situation, as a married woman, is more precarious than Nicholas's she is nevertheless presented as more than willing to enjoy the delights Nicholas can offer, *Whan that she may hir leyser wel espie*. The tone of the passage gives no suggestion that Alisoun is reluctant to commit herself to this illicit relationship, provided that she is not caught by her husband.

In *Edward II*, Marlowe presents Gaveston as a character who is ready to engage in whatever form of manipulation is required to attain his own ends. Edward is vulnerable because of this, particularly in the light of the deep knowledge Gaveston has of him. Edward has the power of a king but also the duties of his position to consider. The effect Gaveston has on the king is developed throughout the play but the audience is alerted here to Edward's vulnerabilities, which obviously lay him open to the machinations of one such as Gaveston.

In *A Woman of No Importance*, Rachel Arbuthnot is also vulnerable and ultimately becomes the victim of an unscrupulous man who refuses to accept his responsibilities. The effect on her, as a woman in Victorian society, is to be left isolated and to make her regard herself as *a guilty thing*. Her behaviour in having a relationship with a man outside marriage was regarded as socially unacceptable; in fact some women in her position chose suicide rather than face the condemnation levelled at them by society. Rachel Arbuthnot's illicit love has a physical manifestation in the form of Gerald, her son. Thus her *sin* can never be forgotten and *She will always suffer*.

Other writers also explore the extent to which illicit sex has a very different outcome for a man than for a woman. Though Hardy presents Sue Bridehead, in *Jude the Obscure*, as outspoken and unorthodox in the novel, the different constraints working upon her and on Jude are very evident. Jude complains that she is not prepared to be honest with him, that she has listened to women who teach others that *they must never admit the full truth to a man*, and even that she is playing *the game of elusiveness*. Even though she and Jude are ordinary working people without a place in Victorian high society to defend (unlike Wilde's Rachel Arbuthnot), Sue's position as a woman in a relationship with a man who is not her husband is still perilous. The behaviour of women such as Arabella (see Notes page 101), who consciously dupes Jude into marriage, could be condoned to an extent, because marriage was the best option open to women, who generally lacked the education and opportunities to earn a good living for themselves. Sue articulates her own vulnerability when she says that she has *nobody to defend me* in a society where a woman's position was linked to that of the men – husband, father, son, brother – in her life.

Not only does Hardy present a relationship between two unmarried people which eventually produces two children, but he makes Sue a mouthpiece for some of the book's most radical views. The tragic outcome is regarded by Sue at the end of the novel as retribution for her challenge to established norms, and she returns to her first husband. But the way Hardy raised these issues about the relations between the sexes caused widespread offence, and his detractors dubbed the book 'Jude the Obscene'. Hardy felt that he was writing truthfully about relationships and marriage, and presenting ways in which they might work more honestly, but a bishop publicly burnt his work – 'probably in his despair at not being able to burn me', Hardy remarked in disgust. The author considered the book 'a moral work', but the negative reaction to it caused him to abandon novel writing.

Activity

How does Hardy present Jude's and Sue's unorthodox opinions on love and marriage in this extract from *Jude the Obscure*?

Discussion

Hardy conveys these views particularly effectively by locating them within the context of the narrative and the characters' own anxieties, rather than examining them through the voice of an intrusive narrator. In fact, in case his reader thinks that he is putting words into his characters' mouths, Hardy has Sue rebuke Jude for being *too sermony* and *lecturing* after Jude's speech on the value of honesty in relationships. Jude asserts that women should be frank about their feelings, flying in the face of accepted conventions of the time. Women's position in society was insecure, especially if they had no man to defend them, as Sue herself implies, so it was small wonder that they often used guile to trap a man into matrimony.

However, the viewpoint which proved most shocking to Hardy's audience was Sue's contention that it was up to her to decide *how I'll live with you, and whether I'll be married or no*. Not only did this arrangement contravene the religious and moral codes of the time, but its impact was especially forceful since it was articulated by a woman, in an age where women's views commanded far less respect than men's.

The word 'romance' cannot be applied to *The Collector* in the way we have looked at it in other passages, but there is a sense in which the extract can be said to reveal passion. This passion, however, is more like obsession, as we see the protagonist pursuing his own twisted desires.

The protagonist captures the object of his obsession through meticulous organization and the flawless execution of a ruthless plan. Fowles makes it clear to the reader that, although the protagonist refuses to acknowledge the driving force behind his obsession, what he wants is to acquire absolute power over an unwilling victim. Fowles describes the moment of capture in language that reveals the protagonist's underlying sexual motives as he says *She was mine, I felt suddenly very excited, I knew I'd done it.*

In some ways the protagonist can be seen to romanticize his reasons for capturing the girl. However, what he refuses to acknowledge is that his passion stems from a selfish desire to possess her like an object, and to have complete control over the destiny of someone who would ordinarily be unattainable to him.

Activity

List the various forms of illicit love shown in the extracts discussed above, and their possible consequences.

Discussion

Homosexual love in *Edward II* is shown to involve the risk of:

- loss of power
- vulnerability
- lack of social acceptance
- ridicule and/or contempt
- imprisonment or, in mediaeval times, the death penalty, often inflicted in a particularly vicious way.

Adulterous love in *The Miller's Tale* risks:

- jealousy
- divorce
- violent retribution
- social exclusion.

Sex before marriage in *A Woman of No Importance* and *Jude the Obscure* risks:

- social exclusion
- lack of future marriage prospects
- self-blame
- banishment from one's own family
- the stigma of illegitimacy
- poverty and physical vulnerability.

The way in which such illicit relationships are presented varies greatly, and this is often to do with the time in which the piece was written. Earlier texts, governed by strict moral and social codes and religious doctrines, often present illicit love as something that should be punished. Some texts, however, use such relationships as a way of highlighting general corruption and moral decay. The relationship between Giovanni and Annabella in *'Tis Pity She's a Whore* is a case in point here.

This is clearly and most obviously an illicit relationship, because they are brother and sister. Writing about such a controversial topic is clearly not without purpose, and John Ford seems to use this extreme situation to explore issues of justice and revenge. In many ways, the relationship between the brother and sister is not the key issue; the judgment of those around them is what is put under the spotlight. It is for this reason that the relationship is presented with simple beauty – *Here's none but you and I* – rather than as something torrid and passionate, in contrast to many other presentations of illicit love in literature through the ages.

Though incest still remains taboo, many modern texts reflect a more relaxed view of many types of sexual relationships, and often a love that some would regard as illicit is used as a narrative tool to hook the reader or reveal certain moral attributes of societies or characters.

Unrequited love

Throughout the ages literature has been full of men and women who have complained that their love is not returned, or not sufficiently valued. Of the many experiences of love, one of the most painful is when individuals surrender themselves either emotionally or physically to partners who cannot or will not reciprocate their feelings. Here we will consider the following extracts:

- *A Woman of No Importance*: Oscar Wilde
- *The Spanish Tragedy*: Thomas Kyd
- *Remember*: Christina Rossetti

Activity

Look at the extract from *A Woman of No Importance* and consider the effect on Rachel Arbuthnot of her unrequited love.

Discussion

The consequences for Rachel Arbuthnot are more far-reaching than just emotional pain. Wilde's play was written at a time when a strict moral code was applied (to women, at least) in sexual matters. For a woman to have a child outside marriage was considered a matter of great shame. Rachel Arbuthnot allows herself to be put into this situation because of her love for Lord Illingworth – *She loved him so much, and he had promised to marry her!* – and it results in a lifetime of concealment and self-blame. In contrast, Illingworth inherits his father's property and is well respected. Thus we see Wilde suggesting that blind faith in love and naive trust can have devastating consequences.

In *The Spanish Tragedy*, Thomas Kyd presents the frustration and anger that unrequited love can bring, and the extract illustrates Balthazar's feelings of despair at Bellimperia's rejection of his advances. Balthazar seems to be torn between self-deprecation and anger towards Bellimperia; first he says that *she is wilder, and more hard withal,/Than beast, or bird, or tree, or stony wall*, and then he checks himself, saying *It is my fault, not she, that merits blame*. Though it is often expected we would sympathize with the person who is being rejected, Kyd makes it difficult for us wholeheartedly to do so here.

There is a more complex presentation of rejection in Christina Rossetti's poem *Remember*. The poem takes the perspective of the person who is rejecting or taking leave of her love, which makes the poem stand out. Rossetti creates an apologetic, sympathetic tone which allows the reader to feel sorry for both parties. Using phrases associated with dying (such as *the silent land* and *the darkness and corruption*) and with mourning also emphasizes the sadness of a failed relationship.

Christina Rossetti, drawn by her brother Dante Gabriel Rossetti in 1866

Meetings and partings

Meetings and partings are crucial moments in a love relationship, and are often portrayed in the literature of love. They can involve many different and complex emotions.

The idea of love at first sight is often featured, and many writers have attempted to capture the passion and excitement of such a moment. Meetings between loved ones can also be used to indicate the future of the relationship and create suspense for the audience.

Many texts deal with the experience of the loss of love, and often develop in the reader sympathy for those left behind. However, the emotions of anger and resentment can also be present, and often writers will challenge the sympathies felt, portraying contradictory feelings of anger and love.

The following extracts look at some of the emotions experienced by various characters in connection with meetings and partings:

- *The Eve of St Agnes*: John Keats
- *Four Letter Word – New Love Letters*: eds Knelman and Porter
- *The Collector*: John Fowles
- *Testament of Youth*: Vera Brittain
- *On My First Daughter*: Ben Jonson
- *Daffodils*: Ted Hughes
- *A Valediction: Forbidding Mourning*: John Donne
- *Letter to Fanny Brawne*: John Keats
- *Dear Scott, Dearest Zelda*: Zelda Fitzgerald

The extract from John Keats's poem *The Eve of St Agnes* presents a highly charged meeting between two lovers, and the consummation of their love.

Activity

Look at the extract from *The Eve of St Agnes* and consider how the presentation of this meeting compares with Chaucer's account of Nicholas and Alisoun's encounter in *The Miller's Tale*.

Discussion

The meeting between Porphyro and Madeline is more emotionally charged than the humorous passage from Chaucer. Keats makes it quite clear, through the use of contrasts, that Porphyro is struggling with his emotions. Unlike Nicholas in Chaucer's tale, Porphyro aims to be true to the image of the romantic lover, so becomes *pale as smooth-sculptured stone* when Madeline awakes, in contrast to the boldness of Nicholas. Madeline's response to Porphyro is again quite different from that of Alisoun to Nicholas. She begins to weep and sees Porphyro as *pallid, chill, and drear*. In the Chaucer passage the consummation is postponed, but Keats conveys it through the use of metaphor and heightened language, with phrases such as *throbbing star, Into her dream he melted* and *Solution sweet.* Unlike in Chaucer's poem, however, the reader is not left with a feeling of Madeline's complicity in this act, as it is presented from the male point of view.

The extract from *Four Letter Word – New Love Letters* is unusual in that it contains the excitement of a first encounter without the two people involved ever really meeting. It is also unusual in that this account is addressed by one of the participants to the other using the second person, as befits a love letter. The text presents tiny details of an occasion when they 'almost' met – even down to *one tiny freckle just above the side of your mouth*. It depicts the writer as completely fascinated by the woman, illustrating the impact of love at first sight. The reflective tone of the narrative is suitable to its context as a memory of the beginning of something that is potentially highly significant. We are given a snapshot of an occasion where little appears to happen outwardly, in contrast to the intensity of the writer's feelings and thoughts about the nature of love. The piece is personal in terms of the insight it gives into the feelings of the writer, yet we learn very little about the woman in question – for us, as for the writer, she remains an enigma.

In *The Collector*, John Fowles presents the reader with a first meeting of a very different kind. This encounter marks the beginning of a relationship between a kidnapper and the young woman who becomes his prey. Miranda, the young woman, is lured into a carefully planned trap and then brutally seized. What this meeting reveals is the vulnerability of Miranda and the perverse obsession with power and ownership of the narrator: *She was mine, I felt suddenly very excited, I knew I'd done it.*

Vera Brittain's *Testament of Youth* presents both an imagined meeting and a final parting, this time through the eyes of a woman. We are given a sensitive account of one woman's expectations of love and her celebration of her complete trust in and commitment to her fiancé. This, and the fact that it is autobiographical writing rather than fiction, makes the passage extremely moving. Brittain's understated style allows the reader to engage with her *tremulous eagerness of anticipation* and, although it is not stated, with what must have been her feeling when the tragic outcome becomes clear.

Ben Jonson's poem *On My First Daughter* also explores the terrible parting at death. But Jonson presents conflicting feelings about death; he holds onto the idea of the death of his daughter as a kind of rebirth where, although she is separated from her parents, they can find comfort in the belief that she is being cared for by the Virgin Mary in heaven. The poem does not deny the pain and suffering of the bereaved parents, but does offer the hope for a life beyond the grave, *In comfort of her mother's tears.*

In Ted Hughes's autobiographical poem *Daffodils*, the final parting between the mother and her family and between husband and wife is more agonizing because there is much less sense of any hope of reunion in heaven: when the poet writes *We knew we'd live forever* he implies that this has been painfully disproved. Functioning as a potent and multi-layered symbol in the poem, the daffodils represent the *fleeting* quality of the narrator's life with his wife. The mother is forgotten by her own child but, poignantly, her *wedding-present scissors… remember. Wherever they are*, their tarnished blades providing *an anchor* amid the deep pain of loss and *a cross of rust* as a memorial to her.

The poet Ted Hughes, who writes about his memories of his wife Sylvia Plath in *Daffodils*

John Donne's poem *A Valediction: Forbidding Mourning*, rather than presenting the trauma of separation, suggests that those who can rise above the often trite emotions associated with missing a loved one are far superior to those *Dull sublunary lovers* who insist on bemoaning it. The poem celebrates the strength of the couple's bond, one that will make them capable of surviving the pain of being apart. The poem is gently humorous in the narrator's playfully arrogant assertions that their relationship is above simple human emotion. This is consolidated by his elevated language (such as *Our two souls… which are one*) and the striking images related to physics and cosmology, which give a sophisticated air to the consolations he is offering.

John Keats's letter to Fanny Brawne gives us an even more emotionally complex view of separation. The letter clearly depicts the stress that separation can cause. Driven by feelings of anxiety and lack of trust, Keats's pain at being separated from his love is very clear.

Activity

Look at the ways in which Keats's anxiety is conveyed in his *Letter to Fanny Brawne*. How is the impact of his separation from her presented in the text?

Discussion

The letter is characterized by an almost melodramatic tone, with hyperbolic descriptions of Keats's pain and suffering, and references to illness and death. Keats makes use of the direct address *you* many times to add a rather accusatory tone. We can feel some sympathy for his plight, as his letter lays bare anxieties that we may all recognize from our own experience, but it is also easy to feel sympathy for the recipient as her trustworthiness is brought into question, and she is told that she is only acceptable in the idealized form of *chaste you; virtuous you*.

In complete contrast to Keats's letter, Zelda Fitzgerald writes what is, in many ways, a traditional love letter, exploring the emotion of being apart. This piece presents the frustration of being separated and the ways such pain can be dealt with. The emotions seen here are quite raw and the impact of the separation is clear. The fact that we are being presented with just one side of the experience makes it difficult for us to relate to both lovers, although the detail of the letter allows us to make some assumptions about the relationship.

Activity

What do you think we learn about the couple and their relationship through Zelda Fitzgerald's letter?

Discussion

- We know that the two are to be married soon, but that they have been separated for some time.
- We also discover that she admires the way he shows his emotions. Her reference to his *melancholy* and *sad tenderness* as

things that she loves tells us that he suffers from feelings of sadness, but that she does not see this as a weakness – rather, it is something she appreciates.

- The description of their arguments as *dear, dear little fusses* could suggest that the two of them argue a lot but that she feels compelled to reassure him their battles do not have real significance.
- Her direct address to him beginning in line 21 also allows us to infer insecurities in Scott. Though she tells him not to fear that he cannot offer her things, the phrasing of the first sentence (*don't ever think of the things you can't give me*) indicates that she does feel there are things he will not be able to offer her.
- The final part of the letter is peppered with references to herself as an object Scott owns, *like a watch-charm*. Though this may suggest that she knows her place within the relationship, it also emphasizes just how willing she is to give herself entirely to the man she loves, and cements our view of the couple's passionate love.

Zelda Fitzgerald and her husband Scott in 1921

Parents and family

The relationship between parent and child involves perhaps one of the most complex forms of love. Some of the extracts look at the ways parents and children respond and interact. While it is not easy being a parent, taking the role of sibling can be even more complicated. We will be looking at the variety of emotions associated with all kinds of familial love in the following texts:

- *One Flesh*: Elizabeth Jennings
- *On My First Daughter*: Ben Jonson
- *A Woman of No Importance*: Oscar Wilde
- *Clearances 5*: Seamus Heaney
- *My Mother*: Jamaica Kincaid
- *The First Tooth*: Mary Lamb

Family members are intimately linked to one another, whether they like it or not; and the fate, behaviour and emotions of some always have an impact on others in a family. While *One Flesh* is first and foremost an examination of the relationship of the poet's parents with each other, a relationship about which the poet is seemingly able to be objective, there is also the sense in the poem that the narrator is assessing the implications for herself in her parents' situation. Observing the ways in which her mother and father are *Strangely apart, yet strangely close together*, and the fact that lack of passion is a feature of their age (*Do they know they're old,/These two who are my father and my mother*), the poet cannot help but be aware of the *new event* whose arrival will rob her of them. Moreover, there is sadness and even resentment in the poet's realization that the *fire from which I came, has now grown cold*.

In *On My First Daughter*, Ben Jonson explores the pain of loss when a child dies. He finds comfort, however, in a firm belief in a benevolent God. The baby has died at the age of six months but the parents hold onto the belief that the child is with God and is being cared for by the blessed Virgin. Thus unlike many other poets writing about the death of a child (see Seamus Heaney's *Mid-term Break*, for example), Jonson presents death as a new beginning rather than an ending, finding some solace that *her innocence* makes the child fit to be part of the Virgin Mary's *virgin train*. A bleaker portrayal of what happens when death separates a parent and very young child is found in *Daffodils*. Here the mother has died but the daughter is too young to remember her. Addressing his dead wife, the poet recalls a happy time for the family, but it is one that their daughter *has forgotten./She cannot even remember you.* While Hughes seems to be indicating that the mother's existence is a blank to the little girl, it is evident that she is alive to the poet himself, since her ghost permeates the whole poem.

The role of the mother is also explored in *A Woman of No Importance*, where Wilde presents us with a woman who has been emotionally scarred by her relationship with the father of her child. In contrast, in *Clearances 5* Seamus Heaney offers a view of his own intimate relationship with his mother while at the same time hinting at the overarching need to *touch and go* – to be close to a parent yet be able to separate oneself at the appropriate time and in the appropriate way.

Activity

Explore the similarities and differences in the extracts from *A Woman of No Importance* and *Clearances 5* in terms of their presentation of parental love.

Discussion

In *A Woman of No Importance* Rachel Arbuthnot is presented as a mother who is unable to separate her own predicament from consideration of her son's future. The audience of the play may well feel that she is right to be very wary of Lord Illingworth's influence on her son, in the light of her experience, but it is her own emotional reactions that – understandably – dominate her long speech here. She uses hyperbolic language to convey her feelings, referring to herself as a *leper* and *a woman who drags a chain like a guilty thing*. The power of her words is reinforced by biblical imagery (such as *no joy, no peace, no atonement*) and the reiteration of the word *ruined*.

She never indicates that the woman she is describing is herself, so her explanation of why she objects to Lord Illingworth seems one-sided to Gerald, and it is not surprising that he wishes to find some excuse as to why Lord Illingworth should behave in such a way towards an unknown woman. In this passage we see a woman who is very reluctant to let go of *mother's own boy*, pouring out to her son her probably long-pent-up emotional reactions without fully explaining the reasons for them.

In contrast Heaney uses an everyday incident to explore in a subtle way the complex relationship between himself and his mother. The fact that he chooses to portray this through the domestic image of the sheets does not hide the emotional nature of the real subject matter. In this short poem Heaney touches on one of the most difficult aspects of the mother–child relationship: the way a mother gives the child enough security to allow him/her to *touch and go* and to be able to come *close again by holding back*. Often it is the words that are unsaid that hold so much more significance than trite expressions of love.

Heaney makes interesting use of the symbols of *X* and *O* to explore the complexity of the relationship. *X* is often used symbolically to represent an unknown person and *O* can be seen both as the womb, a place of safety and also that which is complete, something that has no beginning and end but is smooth and whole. The two symbols are also commonly used in affectionate letters or cards, especially by children, the *X* standing for a kiss, the *O* a hug. Here, they are also used to suggest a game of noughts and crosses, and Heaney attempts to unravel the complex nature of familial love through the image of a game where lines are drawn, turns are taken and there is no outright winner. The chances of both players are equal: it is rarely a game of skill, since chance decides who wins each round. The game can easily be played multiple times and its outcome changes according to circumstance.

A more unusual picture of the relationship between mother and child is presented in *My Mother*. Jamaica Kincaid's story is not one of physical realism but it is rich in psychological meanings, showing the complexities of the mother–daughter relationship as the narrator grows up. The tensions and resentments between them are shown by words such as *pain*, *pity*, *suffocated*, and *sharp glance*. There are powerful images such as the earth being drenched with tears, which eventually form *a small pond*. In particular this extract uses the image of the *bosom* to explore how the mother both nurtures and smothers her daughter until, developing her own breasts, the girl is able to think for herself and be more self-reliant.

Another strikingly different presentation of familial love appears in Mary Lamb's poem *The First Tooth*. Using a child-like style, this poem presents the simplicity of sibling relationships through a brother's and sister's conversation. The petty jealousies and frustrations of the elder sister are shown, but the alliteration

The writer Jamaica Kincaid explores the mother–daughter relationship

in her descriptions of the three causes of her jealousy – the *tiny tooth*, *single sound*, and *mimic motion* – emphasizes the innocent, child-like tone, and the regular rhythm enhances the humour of the situation. It is paradoxically through the rather familiar emotion of jealousy that the love between the two is seen. Lamb uses a conversational tone to create a sense of the relationship between the brother and sister, showing us that the two are close despite the competition between them. This presentation of familial love through humour and familiarity is very simple and engaging.

God, nature and country

From the presentation of a love of God seen in early prayers and hymns, to the passionate love of nature seen in many of the Romantic poets, writers have tried to express feelings of other types of love as well as the love for human beings. The love of one's country has inspired many writers, including Shakespeare, and continues to do so to the present day. The pre-Somme poetry of the First World War was especially characterized by outbursts of patriotic fervour, and stirred many to focus on their relationship with their nation both during the fighting and beyond.

It is interesting to compare the techniques used to reflect these types of love with those used to explore relationships between people, as we often see the same style and form employed and many writers personify a deity, nation or nature in expressing feelings of love towards them. We will look at the following texts for this section:

- *On My First Daughter*: Ben Jonson
- *The Clod and the Pebble*: William Blake
- *Middlemarch*: George Eliot
- *Deo Salvatori*: Thomas Fettiplace
- *Lines composed while climbing the left ascent of Brockley Coomb*: S.T. Coleridge
- *Richard II*: William Shakespeare
- *Henry V*: William Shakespeare

Humanity's love of God has been explored in many ways, but Jonson's poem *On My First Daughter* reveals a belief in a benevolent God in the face of personal tragedy. Here *heaven's queen*, the Virgin Mary, is a real person to the poet rather than an idea. Jonson suggests that his daughter's death signals a rebirth as she is now with Mary, *placed amongst her virgin train* in heaven. In consequence, although the parents grieve for their loss, they take comfort in the thought that their daughter is in a better place and that their child died *With safety of her innocence* rather than being exposed to the dangers of the world.

William Blake is another writer whose relationship with God was a personal rather than intellectual one. In *The Clod and the Pebble*, Blake identifies God with love, though not always in generally accepted ways. He calls conventionally Christian references to mind as he outlines both the selfless and the selfish outworkings of love, and much of this poem paraphrases a passage from the Bible that would have been very familiar to his audience (see Notes pages 81–2). However, although Blake's devotion to his faith was ardent, he interpreted the Bible highly individually. Here he appears to give the Pebble as appealing a voice as the Clod, and to suggest that a selfish possessiveness (as, he suggests elsewhere, was demonstrated by the God of the Old Testament) might lie beneath seeming altruism.

In the extract from *Middlemarch*, George Eliot deals with the outcomes of a love for God, rather than the details of a relationship with God. The writer – real name Mary Ann Evans – had been fiercely evangelical in her teens and, although her religious and philosophical views had changed by the time she wrote *Middlemarch*, her determination to seek a moral foundation for human actions had not left her. In Dorothea Brooke she creates a character with a scrupulous conscience and a need to find moral justification for her decisions in meticulous detail. The narrator in the extract describes Dorothea's personality in detail, commenting directly on the *intensity of her religious disposition*, and describing her nature as *ardent, theoretic, and intellectually consequent*.

Throughout the ages, a love of God was often communicated through prayer, hymns and psalms. The simple forms and direct sentiments used often presented this love as a duty and responsibility rather than a passion. Although the Metaphysical poets such as John Donne and George Herbert wrote religious verses that read like passionate love poems, religious writing was usually not driven by the personal emotions associated with love but by biblical conventions and by a feeling of awe rather than intimacy. The relationship between God and humanity is often seen in literary texts as that of master and servant, though this does not detract from the beauty of the sentiment, as such texts often illustrate devotion and admiration. *Deo Salvatori* by Thomas Fettiplace represents the idea of self-sacrifice as an important element of a love of God. The speaker identifies himself as *Thy servant* and speaks of his *broken heart/Bleeding for sin*; the idea that sin separates a person from God and causes grief is an important one in verse of this type. The poem is a plea for God's *saving grace* and an expression of repentance and self-abasement.

A similar sense of devotion can be seen in literature that reflects a love of nature. This love is presented in many of Samuel Taylor Coleridge's works and, in an echo of many religious poems, he often expresses a sense of awe. His poems illustrate this love through simple description of the landscape. Like many poets from the Romantic movement, in the poem *Lines composed while climbing the left ascent of Brockley Coomb* Coleridge emphasizes his love of the countryside through the prominent use of literary devices such as metaphor and exclamation. He also often employs sound patterns such as alliteration, assonance and sibilance; for example, the birds are *sweet songsters* and the *May-thorn blends its blossoms*. These techniques are familiar in much literature about the sublime power of nature as they evoke the senses and help to make the scene vivid for the reader.

Activity

Look at the two poems from Thomas Fettiplace and S.T. Coleridge. Compare the ways in which the two present their love of God and nature. Are there any similarities in their methods? What may account for the different techniques they employ?

Discussion

- Both texts make use of a first-person narrative, though they employ the structure for different reasons and with different outcomes. Fettiplace addresses God directly in his verse as *Thou* and creates a conversational structure, whereas Coleridge uses the first person in order to reflect his thoughts and feelings as a participant in the scene he is describing.
- Fettiplace uses a simple *aabb* rhyming pattern for a poem that, as with a psalm, takes on the shape and sound of a song. Coleridge's structure is an *abab* pattern, ending with two couplets. The rhythm is iambic pentameter, giving a natural and spontaneous feel to the presentation of his thoughts, as this metre echoes natural speech.
- There is much description and detail about the physical world in *Brockley Coomb* along with the depiction of the speaker's emotions, whereas *Deo Salvatori* is concerned solely with emotions and the relationship to God.
- Both poems refer to *sighs* and use exclamatory phrases, possibly because the principal feeling being expressed by both writers is a sense of awe and of different kinds of sadness, which can be represented by such techniques.

Poets often express their love for nature obliquely, by using imagery from nature to illustrate their ideas. For instance, in *The Clod and the Pebble* Blake explores his theme via the multi-layered images of the *Clod of Clay* and the *Pebble of the brook*, which can be given a variety of interpretations (see Notes page 81). Blake's words are also supported by the visual imagery of his illustrations.

A love for the characteristic landscape and wildlife of Britain often forms the basis for a patriotic love of the country. In many cases town-dwelling writers express their devotion to an idealized British countryside they have experienced only infrequently. Many of the poets of the First World War construct a nation of *flowers, ways* and *rivers*, as Rupert Brooke does in his well-known poem *The Soldier*, to embody a concept for which men might risk their lives. In contrast, in *Testament of Youth*, a memoir of the First World War, a love of one's country is not openly articulated but clearly Roland, like so many other young men of his generation, was prepared to give his life to defend it.

In the extract from *Richard II*, Shakespeare has the dying John of Gaunt describe his country as *This other Eden, demi-paradise... This precious stone set in the silver sea*. Gaunt's speech is not simply a celebration of his love for his country, however, but is an indictment of his nephew Richard's rule over it. It is through the rich and vivid description of the unique characteristics of *This blessed plot* that Gaunt highlights the shortcomings of its ruler. By creating a sense of pride in the *demi-paradise* and its *royal kings... Renowned for their deeds*, Shakespeare explores a criticism of Richard's rule that has remained unarticulated until this point in the play.

Another of Shakespeare's most famous patriotic texts is the *Henry V* speech, where the dramatist uses a range of rhetorical devices to present Henry as both chiding and encouraging his men. Interestingly, there is scant mention of the country for which the characters are fighting. Henry's central theme here is the honour that inspires men to fight even when the odds are stacked against them, and to rebuff the assistance of any who are not with them heart and soul. The love celebrated here is the comradely love of soldiers in arms who are facing terrible danger together in a common cause; Henry repeats the inclusive *we* and emphasizes that they will become a *band of brothers*. He tells them they will have reason for boasting years after their exploits on this day, and that their names will be celebrated *to the ending of the world*. Shakespeare also associates patriotism and soldierly virtues with masculinity, as Henry claims that the non-combatants will *think themselves accursed they were not here,/And hold their manhoods cheap*.

While Shakespeare writes of an England in the midst of war, a war which was to define the nation's spirit, George Eliot examines the state of England at times (both when the book was set and when she was writing it) of internal reform in the country. Coming from the Midlands herself, she understood how provincial towns operated and the types of opinions to be found in the people. *Middlemarch* as a whole presents a range of characters from different backgrounds who represent a microcosm of mid-nineteenth-century society. In the years when Eliot was writing the book, Britain had undergone and was still undergoing fundamental social change caused by industrialization, and many people found themselves in a state of moral and spiritual turmoil as religious certainties were questioned. Dorothea hints at this state of confusion and constant change as she demands of herself: *What could she do, what ought she to do?* and wonders how England can be an appropriate stage on which to *lead a grand life*.

Activity

Compare the ways the extracts from *Henry V* and *Middlemarch* relate to a love of God or country.

Discussion

It is interesting that in Henry V's speech in the play and Dorothea Brooke's musings in *Middlemarch* both characters respond to their situations in an unexpected way. Henry is reacting to the despondency of his generals and the half-heartedness of some of his troops as they see the enemy numbers. Shakespeare's protagonist can confidently deal with these feelings by appealing to the instincts and emotions that lie beneath patriotism and comradely love – a sense of honour and the distinctive features of male, military identity. Defending the country also involves defending one's relationship to God; Henry's speech begins with the exclamation *God's peace*.

Middlemarch was written at a time when England was no less sure of its importance on the world stage but uncertain of the moral framework that should underpin its actions. Living in an environment characterized by complacency and small-mindedness, Dorothea is shown beginning to grasp the nature of this crisis at this early stage in the book and is seeking a path that will fulfil her own spiritual and intellectual ambitions as well as glorify her country and her God.

Style and genre

When studying and comparing extracts such as those in this book, you need to consider the writers' choices of form, structure and language and how these help to communicate the ideas and feelings that concern the writer. It is *how* a writer conveys his or her ideas that chiefly distinguishes one from another. The methods a writer selects help to produce her or his own unique style of writing. It is important to be clear about the different aspects of style that are typical of the three main genres of writing: drama, poetry and prose.

Drama

The drama texts that have come down to us from the time of Shakespeare and his contemporaries tend not to include lengthy stage directions. Theatrical scenery was not widely used in Shakespeare's day, and audiences were dependent on the language used to create the scenes. Hence the presentation of characters' thoughts, feelings and actions relies heavily on the use of poetic devices and in particular the use of vivid imagery. Thus in *Richard II*, John of Gaunt's emotional celebration of his love for England is characterized by metaphor and simile (see Notes page 64). This is also true of Christopher Marlowe's presentation of Gaveston's sensual description of those delights he believes most please his king. Marlowe also uses classical references to complement his images of sensual enjoyment. In contrast, the extract from

Richard II relies more heavily on rhetoric and at times uses synecdoche to express Gaunt's emotional connection with England. As with many other writers, Shakespeare draws on biblical references to add power to a speech.

With both Shakespeare and Marlowe the clues about characters' emotions are contained in the form and structure of the language used. This is also true of Thomas Kyd, and Balthazar's anger and frustration are made clear through the cyclical and repetitive nature of his speech in the extract from *The Spanish Tragedy*. These techniques replace what in prose might be the authorial voice or the omniscient narrator, as we learn about the characters from what they say and how they say it. Characters both interact with one another in rapid conversations and are given long speeches and soliloquies in which to express their ideas and feelings to the audience.

The soliloquy is a technique frequently associated with sixteenth-century dramatists but is still seen in some modern drama. As the character is alone on the stage and speaking only to himself or herself, it is reasonable to assume that the words uttered convey complete frankness. In *Edward II*, Gaveston's description of how he sees his relationship with the king, and the deep knowledge he has of Edward, is designed to reveal the form Edward's and Gaveston's relationship will take. We also obtain insight into Giovanni's emotional distress and conflicting desires in the soliloquy that opens the extract from *'Tis Pity She's a Whore*, giving the audience the chance to engage with his plight.

By the end of the nineteenth century, scenery, props and detailed stage directions were more popular and the setting of *A Woman of No Importance*, for example, was lavish, in keeping with the high society Wilde is challenging. The stage directions seen in the extract allow Wilde to foreground the power Mrs Arbuthnot has over her son as well as her tenderness for him: *Gerald sits down beside his mother. She runs her fingers through his hair, and strokes his hands*. This apparent dominance is reaffirmed in the fact that Mrs Arbuthnot is given most of the dialogue. However, what is unusual about the exchange between Gerald

The playwright Oscar Wilde, in a sketch of 1895

and his mother is that, although Gerald speaks very little, his patronizing tone and unforgiving response serve to silence Mrs Arbuthnot and shift the power to him.

Wilde tends to use rhetorical devices, particularly tripling, to build up tension and add force to an argument, for example in the lines *She suffered terribly – she suffers now. She will always suffer.* He also makes use of the rhetorical device of repetition, such as of the word *suffer* here and *ruined* elsewhere in the extract, to emphasize the tragedy of Mrs Arbuthnot's position. Dramatic pauses such as the one at line 45, and the use of short, staccato sentences, all serve to build up tension.

Poetry

Poetry can express emotion in a concentrated way and can take a variety of forms. A poem may be a sonnet, with its fourteen-line form, or a ballad which echoes the form and techniques of a song, or it may be a narrative poem, which is usually longer and possibly written in blank verse. Much modern poetry is written as free verse, rather than in any of these traditional formats. On the whole, all poetry is characterized by the use of figurative language or tropes such as similes, metaphors, and personification, and by rhetorical devices including alliteration, assonance and onomatopoeia.

When studying any poem, you should consider what effect was intended by the writer when a particular device is employed. Certain styles may be considered to lend themselves well to the presentation of the emotions associated with love and so have, throughout time, been used to explore the topic. Shakespeare's use of the sonnet structure and Carol Ann Duffy's use of dramatic monologue in many of her works about love are examples of this.

Rhyme is important in many poems. In Seamus Heaney's poem *Clearances 5* the rhyme scheme is unobtrusive, yet complements the simplicity of the action he is describing. Similar techniques can be seen in Duffy's work, where half-rhymes and internal rhymes are often a feature. The simple rhyme and metrical scheme resembling that of a hymn in Blake's *The Clod and the Pebble* gives impact to the writer's message, as well as giving the poem appropriate religious connotations.

Keats's poem *The Eve of St Agnes* is a narrative poem told like a story. It has an ordered pattern of nine-line stanzas, with an *ababbcbcc* rhyme scheme. This patterning helps to create the atmosphere of a romance or fairytale. The rhythm is basically iambic pentameter (a ten-syllable line with the stress falling on every second syllable); this is the pattern used by many poets but it is particularly noticeable in the works of Shakespeare and his contemporaries.

Keats's work is characterized by rich colour imagery (such as *azure-lidded* and *blanchèd*), and sensual language; we read of *lustrous salvers* and *voluptuous accents*. These are contrasted with *iced stream* and *smooth-sculptured stone* to achieve an effect of passion and desire balanced by purity and innocence. Like many poets, Keats uses the pathetic fallacy as he describes the *frost-wind* and the *sharp sleet* that demonstrate the dangers of the outside world, as well as the metaphorical pain of reality in contrast to the dreaming world of *woofèd fantasies*.

Coleridge employs similar techniques in order to evoke the sense of the sublime he experiences in the presence of nature. His work, like that of many other poets who explore the emotions of love, reflects his passion through the use of intensifiers, exclamations and phrases that evoke the senses, such as *Ah! what a luxury of landscape meets/My gaze!*

Prose

Just like poetry, prose can take a variety of forms: a novel like *The Collector* may be written as first-person narrative although it is clearly fictional, while *Testament of Youth*, although also written in the first person, is a non-fiction autobiographical account of one woman's experiences during the First World War. Just as with poetry, prose writers adopt a variety of figurative devices to convey meaning and atmosphere. In *The Collector*, John Fowles chooses to use colloquial language to build up a picture in the reader's mind of the way the main character thinks and speaks. In contrast, Brittain chooses a more elevated style which reflects her own class, education and subject matter.

The creation of the narrative voice is crucial. In the extract from *Jane Eyre*, for example, we are presented with a confident and self-assured female protagonist. This frames our engagement with the relationship being presented. In the extract from *Four Letter Word – New Love Letters*, Matthew Zapruder similarly uses the narrative voice to shape our experience of the person being portrayed; his rather whimsical, intriguing protagonist paints a humorous image of the couple's first meeting, an image that instantly appeals, drawing us into the relationship.

Earlier prose writers such as George Eliot or Thomas Hardy often prefer to use an omniscient narrator, which may have the effect of distancing the audience from the characters, enabling the reader to view their actions and feelings more clearly. Such narrators occasionally intrude into the narrative, presenting their own point of view, making a judgement or detailing a moral stance – which may stimulate further speculation about the characters and events. Eliot does this with her description of the moral nature of Dorothea Brooke in *Middlemarch*, especially in the comments on the contentment Dorothea might have achieved if she had *some endowment of stupidity and conceit… From such contentment poor Dorothea was shut out.*

Sometimes the narrative voice of an author assumes a restricted view, as Thomas Hardy does in the extract from *Jude the Obscure*, where he details the conversation of the two lovers without much direct comment, and mostly from Jude's point of view.

In studying works of any genre in the literature of love from any age, then, it is important to pay attention to *how* the author gets across ideas and feelings; you also need to consider the point of view from which these ideas come, the voice in which they are articulated, and the language features that help to make the writing vivid and meaningful.

Essay Questions

1 Look again at Shakespeare's *Sonnet 18* and Carol Ann Duffy's *First Love.* Basing your answer on the poems and, where appropriate, your wider reading in the poetry of love, compare the ways the two poets have used poetic form, structure and language to express their thoughts and ideas.

2 Focusing on John Donne's *A Valediction: Forbidding Mourning* and Christina Rossetti's *Remember*, write a comparison of the ways the writers present the partings of people who love each other.
You should consider:
- the ways the writers' choices of form, structure and language shape your responses to these poems
- how your wider reading in the literature of love has contributed to your understanding and interpretation of the poems.

3 Look again at Ben Jonson's *On My First Daughter* and Douglas Dunn's *The Kaleidoscope.* Basing your answer on the poems and, where appropriate, your wider reading in the poetry of love, compare the ways the two poets have used poetic form, structure and language to express their thoughts and ideas.

4 Focusing on the extract from Thomas Kyd's *The Spanish Tragedy* and John Keats's *Letter to Fanny Brawne*, write a comparison of the ways the writers present unrequited love.
You should consider:
- the ways the writers' choices of form, structure and language shape your responses to these extracts
- how your wider reading in the literature of love has contributed to your understanding and interpretation of the extracts.

5 Basing your answer on the extract from Shakespeare's *Richard II* and S.T. Coleridge's poem *Lines composed while climbing the left ascent of Brockley Coomb* as well as, where

appropriate, your wider reading in the poetry of love, compare the ways the two poets have used poetic form, structure and language to express their thoughts and ideas.

6 Look again at the extract from Charlotte Brontë's *Jane Eyre* and Douglas Dunn's *The Kaleidoscope.* Write a comparison of the ways the writers present marriage.
You should consider:
- the ways the writers' choices of form, structure and language shape your responses to these extracts
- how your wider reading in the literature of love has contributed to your understanding and interpretation of the extracts.

7 Focusing on the extracts from Shakespeare's *Much Ado About Nothing* and John Ford's *'Tis Pity She's A Whore*, write a comparison of the ways the writers present romantic love.
You should consider:
- the ways the writers' choices of form, structure and language shape your responses to these extracts
- how your wider reading in the literature of love has contributed to your understanding and interpretation of the extracts.

8 Focusing on the extracts from *Four Letter Word: New Love Letters* and John Fowles's *The Collector*, write a comparison of the ways the writers present the meetings of their characters.
You should consider:
- the ways the writers' choices of form, structure and language shape your responses to these extracts
- how your wider reading in the literature of love has contributed to your understanding and interpretation of the extracts.

9 Look again at the extracts from Geoffrey Chaucer's *The Miller's Tale* and John Keats's *The Eve of St Agnes*. Basing your answer on the passages and, where appropriate, your wider reading in the poetry of love, compare the ways the

two poets have used poetic form, structure and language to express their thoughts and ideas.

10 Focusing on Seamus Heaney's poem *Clearances 5* and Ben Jonson's *On My First Daughter*, write a comparison of the ways the writers present the parent–child relationship.
You should consider:

- the ways the writers' choices of form, structure and language shape your responses to these poems
- how your wider reading in the literature of love has contributed to your understanding and interpretations of the poems.

11 Look again at William Blake's *The Clod and the Pebble* and Shakespeare's *Sonnet 18*. Basing your answer on the passages and, where appropriate, your wider reading in the poetry of love, compare the ways the two poets have used poetic form, structure and language to express their thoughts and ideas.

12 Focusing on the extracts from Oscar Wilde's *A Woman of No Importance* and Christopher Marlowe's *Edward II*, write a comparison of the ways the writers present illicit love.
You should consider:

- the ways the writers' choices of form, structure and language shape your responses to these extracts
- how your wider reading in the literature of love has contributed to your understanding and interpretations of the extracts.

13 Basing your answer on the extract from Vera Brittain's *Testament of Youth* and on Elizabeth Jennings's *One Flesh* and, where appropriate, your wider reading in the literature of love, compare the ways the two writers have used form, structure and language to express their thoughts and ideas.

14 Look again at the extracts from John Fowles's *The Collector* and John Keats's *Letter to Fanny Brawne*, and write a comparison of the ways the writers present possessive love.

You should consider:

- the ways the writers' choices of form, structure and language shape your responses to these extracts
- how your wider reading in the literature of love has contributed to your understanding and interpretations of the extracts.

15 Look again at Christina Rossetti's *Remember* and Ted Hughes's *Daffodils*. Basing your answer on these poems, and where appropriate, your wider reading in the poetry of love, compare the ways the two poets have used poetic form, structure and language to express their thoughts and ideas.

16 Focusing on the extracts from George Eliot's *Middlemarch* and Thomas Hardy's *Jude the Obscure*, write a comparison of the ways the writers present attitudes to marriage.

You should consider:

- the ways the writers' choices of form, structure and language shape your responses to these extracts
- how your wider reading in the literature of love has contributed to your understanding and interpretations of the extracts.

17 Look again at Carol Ann Duffy's *Pygmalion's Bride* and the extract from *Dear Scott, Dearest Zelda*. Basing your answer on these extracts and, where appropriate, your wider reading in the literature of love, compare the ways the two writers have used form, structure and language to express their thoughts and ideas.

18 Focusing on the extracts from Shakespeare's *Henry V* and *Antony & Cleopatra*, write a comparison of the ways Shakespeare presents the public and political aspects of love.

You should consider:

- the ways Shakespeare's choices of form, structure and language shape your responses to these extracts

- how your wider reading in the literature of love has contributed to your understanding and interpretation of the extracts.

19 Focusing on Ben Jonson's *On My First Daughter* and Thomas Fettiplace's *Deo Salvatori*, write a comparison of the ways the writers present the love of God.
You should consider:
- the ways the writers' choices of form, structure and language shape your responses to these poems
- how your wider reading in the literature of love has contributed to your understanding and interpretation of the poems.

20 Focusing on Mary Lamb's *The First Tooth* and the extract from Jamaica Kincaid's *My Mother*, write a comparison of the ways the writers present familial love.
You should consider:
- the ways the writers' choices of form, structure and language shape your responses to these extracts
- how your wider reading in the literature of love has contributed to your understanding and interpretation of the extracts.

Chronology

The following are some of the most well-known writers who have written about love through the ages.

c. 1343–1400	Geoffrey Chaucer	*The Canterbury Tales, Troilus and Criseyde*
c. 1405–1471	Sir Thomas Malory	*Le Morte d'Arthur*
c. 1552–1599	Edmund Spenser	*The Faerie Queene*
1554–1586	Sir Philip Sidney	*Astrophel and Stella*
1558–1594	Thomas Kyd	*The Spanish Tragedy*
1564–1616	William Shakespeare	*Plays, Sonnets, Venus and Adonis, A Lover's Complaint*
1564–1593	Christopher Marlowe	*Dr Faustus, Edward II, Tamburlaine the Great*
1572–1637	Ben Jonson	*Epicoene, Volpone, Epigrams, The Forest*
1572–1631	John Donne	*Songs and Sonnets, Elegies, Holy Sonnets*
c. 1578–1634	John Webster	*The White Devil, The Duchess of Malfi*
1586–1640	John Ford	*'Tis Pity She's a Whore, The Lady's Trial*
1608–1674	John Milton	*Paradise Lost, Paradise Regained*
c. 1640–1689	Aphra Behn	*The Rover, The Forced Marriage, Love Letters between a Nobleman and his Sister*
c. 1640–1715	William Wycherley	*The Country Wife*
c. 1660–1731	Daniel Defoe	*Moll Flanders*
1670–1729	William Congreve	*The Way of the World*

1689–1761	Samuel Richardson	*Pamela, Clarissa*
1707–1754	Henry Fielding	*The History of Tom Jones, a Foundling*
1730–1774	Oliver Goldsmith	*She Stoops to Conquer*
1751–1816	Richard Brinsley Sheridan	*The Rivals, The School for Scandal*
1757–1827	William Blake	*Songs of Innocence and of Experience*
1759–1796	Robert Burns	*Tam O'Shanter*
1775–1817	Jane Austen	*Northanger Abbey, Sense and Sensibility, Pride and Prejudice, Mansfield Park, Emma, Persuasion*
1788–1824	Lord Byron	*Don Juan*
1795–1821	John Keats	*Lamia, The Eve of St Agnes, Odes, La Belle Dame Sans Merci*
1806–1861	Elizabeth Barrett Browning	*Sonnets from the Portuguese*
1812–1870	Charles Dickens	*The Old Curiosity Shop, Dombey and Son, David Copperfield, Bleak House, Hard Times, A Tale of Two Cities, Great Expectations*
1816–1855	Charlotte Brontë	*Jane Eyre, Shirley, Villette, The Professor, Poems*
1818–1848	Emily Brontë	*Wuthering Heights, Poems*

1819–1880	George Eliot	*The Mill on the Floss, Silas Marner, Middlemarch, Daniel Deronda*
1840–1928	Thomas Hardy	*Under the Greenwood Tree, Far from the Madding Crowd, The Mayor of Casterbridge, Tess of the d'Urbervilles, Jude the Obscure, Poems*
1854–1900	Oscar Wilde	*The Picture of Dorian Gray, A Woman of No Importance, An Ideal Husband, The Importance of Being Earnest*
1879–1970	E.M. Forster	*A Room with a View, Howard's End, Maurice, A Passage to India*
1885–1930	D.H. Lawrence	*Sons and Lovers, The Rainbow, Women in Love, Lady Chatterley's Lover*
1890–1979	Jean Rhys	*Wide Sargasso Sea*
1899–1973	Noel Coward	*Private Lives*
1903–1966	Evelyn Waugh	*Brideshead Revisited*
1904–1991	Graham Greene	*Brighton Rock, The End of the Affair, The Human Factor*
1911–1983	Tennessee Williams	*The Glass Menagerie, A Streetcar Named Desire, Cat on a Hot Tin Roof*

1919–1999	Iris Murdoch	*The Bell*
1922–1985	Philip Larkin	*The Whitsun Weddings*
1924–1995	Robert Bolt	*A Man for All Seasons*
1926–2005	John Fowles	*The Collector, The French Lieutenant's Woman*
1930–1998	Ted Hughes	*Birthday Letters*
1931–	Toni Morrison	*Beloved*
1932–1963	Sylvia Plath	*Ariel*
1936–	A.S. Byatt	*Possession*
1940–1992	Angela Carter	*The Magic Toyshop, Wise Children*
1941–	Anne Tyler	*The Amateur Marriage*
1942–	Susan Hill	*Strange Meeting, The Woman in Black*
1943–	Michael Ondaatje	*The English Patient*
1944–	Alice Walker	*The Color Purple*
1954–	Kazuo Ishiguro	*The Remains of the Day*
1955–	Carol Ann Duffy	*Mean Time, The World's Wife*
1956–	Andrea Levy	*Small Island*
1959–	Jeanette Winterson	*Oranges Are Not the Only Fruit, The Passion, Written on the Body, Gut Symmetries*
1963–	Audrey Niffenegger	*The Time Traveler's Wife*

1965–	Khaled Hosseini	*The Kite Runner, A Thousand Splendid Suns*
1966–	Sarah Waters	*Tipping the Velvet, Fingersmith*
1967–	Monica Ali	*Brick Lane*
1975–	Zadie Smith	*On Beauty*